YoungWriters 2005

PLAYGROU

Let your creativity flow...

ode
limerick
haiku
rhyme
ballad

# Hampshire

Edited by Bobby Tobolik

 Young**Writers**

First published in Great Britain in 2005 by:
Young Writers
Remus House
Coltsfoot Drive
Peterborough
PE2 9JX
Telephone: 01733 890066
Website: www.youngwriters.co.uk

SB ISBN 1 84602 124 3

# Foreword

Young Writers was established in 1991 and has been passionately devoted to the promotion of reading and writing in children and young adults ever since. The quest continues today. Young Writers remains as committed to the fostering of burgeoning poetic and literary talent as ever.

This year's Young Writers competition has proven as vibrant and dynamic as ever and we are delighted to present a showcase of the best poetry from across the UK. Each poem has been carefully selected from a wealth of *Playground Poets* entries before ultimately being published in this, our thirteenth primary school poetry series.

Once again, we have been supremely impressed by the overall high quality of the entries we have received. The imagination, energy and creativity which has gone into each young writer's entry made choosing the best poems a challenging and often difficult but ultimately hugely rewarding task - the general high standard of the work submitted amply vindicating this opportunity to bring their poetry to a larger appreciative audience.

We sincerely hope you are pleased with our final selection and that you will enjoy *Playground Poets Hampshire* for many years to come.

# Contents

William Read  (10)  15
Ben Giles  (10)  15
Megan Fright  (10)  16
Alice Henderson  (10)  16
Danielle Wood  (8)  17
Richard Park  (10)  17
Connor Stewart  (10)  17
Amy Berntsen  (10)  18
Francis Dredge-Hetherington  (11)  18
Connor McCallum  (10)  18

## Castle Hill Junior School

Michaela Andrews  (8)  19
Liberty Barrett  (9)  19
Chloe Lacy  (8)  20
Jade-Marie Hide  (9)  20
Nathan Oliver  (9)  20
Natasha Hudson  (8)  21
Carl Gardiner  (8)  21
Corran Kingsbury  (9)  21
Olivia Willis  (8)  22
Naomi Jones  (8)  22
Samuel Genovese  (9)  22
Vashist Motkur  (9)  23
Sydney White  (9)  23
Jacob Brown  (9)  23
Beverley Stainer  (9)  24
Patrik Toobe  (9)  24
Wade Vince  (9)  24
Lori-Ann Wyatt  (8)  25
Lauren Ludlow  (9)  25
Sam Fettin  (8)  26
Charlie Hannah  (9)  26

## Cove Junior School

Suzi Goose  (11)  26
Charlie Long  (11)  27
Andrew Dyos  (9)  27
Caris Brooks  (10)  28
Marcus Gale  (10)  28
Ryan Cook  (11)  29

| | |
|---|---|
| Paige Gibbons  (9) | 30 |
| Alexandra Davis  (11) | 30 |
| Michael Salter  (11) | 31 |
| Emily Regan  (10) | 31 |
| Laura Pammer  (11) | 32 |
| Ailsa Winter  (10) | 32 |
| Ryan Walters  (10) | 32 |
| Hayden Orriss  (10) | 33 |
| Matthew Casey & Jamie Dawkins  (11) | 33 |
| Sophie Eynon  (11) | 34 |
| Chloe Gray  (10) | 35 |
| Chloë Rogers  (9) | 36 |
| Lucy Irving  (10) | 36 |
| Ryan Hughes  (10) | 37 |
| William Campos  (11) | 37 |
| Jasmine Blair  (11) | 38 |
| Sophie Lynch  (10) | 38 |
| James Lalor  (11) | 39 |
| Anna Stevens  (9) | 39 |
| Mark Haffenden  (9) | 40 |
| Emily Sanders  (11) | 41 |
| Leanne Beales  (10) | 42 |
| Joshua Bouette  (10) | 42 |
| Matthew Webster  (11) | 43 |
| Kimberley Maunders  (9) | 43 |
| Alex Schofield  (9) | 44 |
| Michael Whicker  (11) | 44 |
| Ryan Collingham  (11) | 45 |
| Rosie Chambers  (11) | 46 |
| Emily Coxhead  (11) | 46 |
| Joe Hardy  (11) | 47 |
| Kudzai Sitima  (9) | 47 |
| Jack Hoggard  (9) | 48 |

## Marchwood Junior School

| | |
|---|---|
| Ashley Noyce  (9) | 48 |
| Carissa Bowen  (9) | 49 |
| Jordie Scott  (9) | 49 |
| Matthew Hill  (9) | 50 |
| Sarah Alford  (8) | 50 |
| Emma Stokes  (9) | 51 |

| | |
|---|---:|
| Hannah Reader  (8) | 51 |
| Vilisi Tekei  (9) | 52 |
| Emma Poulton  (8) | 52 |
| Laura Bradford  (8) | 52 |
| Emily Macdonald  (8) | 53 |
| Leila Clelland  (9) | 53 |
| Jimmy McHugh  (9) | 53 |
| Emily Hinton  (8) | 54 |
| Jenny White  (9) | 54 |
| Sophie Manser  (8) | 55 |
| Holly Swanton  (9) | 55 |
| Elizabeth Seary  (9) | 56 |
| Emily Campion  (8) | 56 |
| Beth Harney  (9) | 56 |
| Sally Pitcher  (8) | 57 |
| Calem Amminin  (8) | 57 |
| Sian Sayce  (9) | 57 |
| Joseph Whitfield  (8) | 58 |
| Tyler Burgin  (8) | 58 |
| Joe White  (9) | 59 |
| Laura Rangecroft  (8) | 59 |
| Chelsea Ayres  (9) | 60 |
| Stacey Pettman  (9) | 60 |
| Chloe Meredith & Amy Pickford  (9) | 61 |
| Shanice Lund  (9) | 61 |
| Elliot Ireland  (9) | 62 |
| Sarah White  (8) | 62 |
| Jamie Passfield  (8) | 62 |

**Marycourt School**

| | |
|---|---:|
| Harvey Meeds  (10) | 63 |
| Alex Sharp  (9) | 63 |
| Annabelle Mackay  (9) | 64 |
| Charis White  (10) | 64 |
| Madison Roberts  (8) | 65 |
| Jack Willetts  (8) | 65 |
| Jake Dicken  (9) | 65 |
| Robin White  (8) | 66 |
| Andrew Vincent  (9) | 66 |
| Thomas Battersby  (9) | 67 |
| Ben Lewis  (10) | 67 |

Joe Podmore  (10)       67
Yiannis Panou  (9)       68

## Newbridge Junior School

Bethany Goodchild  (11)       68
Rhiannon Smithard  (11)       69
Thomas Arnfeld (10)       70
Katie Heap  (11)       70
Melissa Peck  (11)       71
Yasmin Wells  (11)       72
Madeline Goodchild  (11)       73
Amber Privett  (10)       74
Samantha Chearman  (11)       75
Vuyani Ncube  (10)       76
Jordan Jones  (11)       77
Jamie Hale  (10)       78

## Portway Junior School

Jacob Morrison  (9)       78
Jack Copping  (8)       79
Ben Cox  (8)       79
Ella Howells  (8)       80
Henry Edwards  (8)       80
James Duff (9)       80
Sophie Roberts       81
Charlie Blackmore  (10)       81
Gillian Parker  (9)       82
Luke Robbins  (9)       82
James Holder  (9)       83
Christopher Speed  (8)       83
Anna-Leigh Brookes  (8)       84
Lewis Parkinson  (9)       84
Lewis Nicholls  (8)       84
Kerry Rookes  (9)       85
Carmen Broome  (8)       85
Ashleigh Gurd  (11)       86
Emma Hine  (10)       86
Zoe Russell (8)       87
Amy Cutting  (10)       87
Anna Bazzoni  (8)       87
Amy Potts  (8)       88

| | |
|---|---:|
| Jeanette Treacy  (8) | 88 |
| Owen Young  (11) | 89 |
| Victoria Collyer  (10) | 89 |
| Bena Tymms  (10) | 90 |
| Sarah Shehata  (9) | 90 |
| Caelan Burnett  (8) | 90 |
| Jordan O'Connor  (10) | 91 |
| Christopher Tanner  (8) | 91 |
| Amanda Brown  (9) | 91 |
| Cristina Trowbridge  (10) | 92 |
| Mitchell Webber  (9) | 92 |
| Kayleigh Lewis  (10) | 93 |
| Kim Willis  (9) | 93 |
| Floyd Steele  (8) | 94 |
| Chelsey Goddard  (9) | 94 |
| Luis Zeffertt  (10) | 94 |
| Joseph Lindridge  (9) | 95 |
| Bradley Buckwell  (9) | 95 |
| Luke Ginger  (10) | 96 |
| Jack Healy  (8) | 96 |
| Rachel Suffling  (11) | 97 |
| Hope Turner  (10) | 97 |
| Liam Williams  (10) | 97 |
| Jade Donnelly  (9) | 98 |
| Tom Beaton  (10) | 98 |
| Imogen George  (10) | 98 |
| Hayley Williamson  (9) | 99 |
| Hannah Fretton  (10) | 99 |
| Chloe Mack  (10) | 100 |
| Liam Williams (10) and James Pitt  (9) | 100 |
| Samuel Hunt  (11) | 101 |
| Nicola Fletcher  (11) | 101 |
| Shannon Goy  (11) | 101 |
| Jack Barrett  (11) | 102 |
| Andrea Kershaw  (10) | 102 |
| Katie Brown  (11) | 102 |
| Thomas Hunt  (11) | 103 |
| Jamie Batchelor  (11) | 103 |
| Richard Lowe  (10) | 103 |
| Kate Mee  (10) | 104 |
| Sian Sorensen  (11) | 104 |
| Kieron Dolan  (11) | 105 |

| | |
|---|---|
| Shaun Wilson (10) | 105 |
| Ashley Brown (10) | 105 |
| Georgia Loftus (10) | 106 |
| Murray Yelf (11) | 106 |
| Archie Sturt (10) | 107 |
| Kenneth Gates (10) | 107 |

## Rookesbury Park School

| | |
|---|---|
| Imogen Savage (8) | 108 |
| Masahiro Nishikawa (7) | 108 |
| Jack Keogh (7) | 108 |
| Anna Cooke (8) | 109 |
| Lydie Stephenson (7) | 109 |
| Katherine Young (7) | 109 |
| Chloe Pleydell (8) | 110 |
| Alistair Main (8) | 110 |
| Maddie Falconer (7) | 111 |
| Joseph Hawkins (7) | 111 |
| Beatrix Bates (9) | 111 |
| Hector Butcher (7) | 112 |
| Rowan Golland (8) | 112 |
| Alexander White (8) | 112 |
| Abigail Guy (9) | 113 |
| Camilla Longman (9) | 113 |
| Heidi Sidorina (10) | 114 |
| Olivia Bowman (10) | 114 |
| Kate Falconer (10) | 115 |
| Charlotte Woodhouse (8) | 115 |
| Laurence Golland (10) | 116 |
| Lauren Norton (11) | 116 |
| Jade Hurley (10) | 117 |
| Samuel Earle (10) | 117 |
| Philippa Blunden (10) | 118 |
| Alex Chandler (11) | 118 |
| Emily Benson-Rhodes (11) | 119 |

## Rucstall Primary School

| | |
|---|---|
| Joseph Scandrett (9) | 119 |
| Jack Verling (9) | 119 |
| Paige Hollis (8) | 120 |
| Lauren Kelly (9) | 120 |

| | |
|---|---:|
| Christy Paul  (9) | 120 |
| Alexander Goodall  (11) | 121 |
| Reece Chapman  (10) | 121 |
| Emma-Louise McCarthy  (9) | 121 |
| Adam Gough  (11) | 122 |
| Amy Jones  (10) | 122 |
| Matthew Goodall  (9) | 123 |
| Christopher Rolfe  (10) | 123 |
| Lewis Greenhalf  (11) | 124 |
| Samantha Coulbeck  (10) | 124 |
| Cavan Reid  (8) | 124 |
| Stephanie Rounce  (10) | 125 |
| Emily West  (10) | 125 |
| Naomi Cole  (10) | 125 |
| Ruhee Padhiar  (11) | 126 |
| Michael Paul  (11) | 126 |
| Greg Donaldson  (11) | 127 |
| Conor Reid  (10) | 127 |
| Joshua Kinderman  (11) | 128 |
| Holly Linehan  (11) | 128 |
| Luke Stratton  (10) | 129 |

## St Paul's Catholic Primary School, Portsmouth

| | |
|---|---:|
| Amy Brockway  (11) | 129 |
| Ebony Adolphe  (11) | 130 |
| Jayne Cummings  (11) | 130 |
| Ellie-Louise Brown  (10) | 130 |
| Jamie Francalanza  (10) | 131 |
| Sarrah Agulan  (10) | 131 |
| Nicole Sainty  (10) | 132 |
| Josh Duff, Alfie Gawn & Danny Mooney  (10) | 132 |
| Hollie Jeans  (10) | 132 |
| Rosalind Waite  (10) | 133 |
| Carmen Langworthy  (11) | 133 |
| Scarlett Robinson  (10) | 134 |
| Sean Burby  (11) | 134 |
| Callum Veale  (10) | 135 |
| Paul Hooper  (11) | 135 |
| Lucy-Ann Catterall  (10) | 136 |
| Molly Jackson  (7) | 136 |
| Eleanor Ransford  (9) | 137 |

Harry Haskett  (9)    161
Samuel Kind  (10)    161
Cormac Dreelan  (9)    162
Gail Sabadera  (7)    162
Imogen Rose  (9)    163
Chloe Rye-Kerr  (9)    163
Nathan Cripps  (9)    164
Holly Duckett  (9)    164
Brett Togwell  (9)    165
Ryan Morgan  (9)    165
Siân Doherty  (9)    166
Jacob Adolphe  (9)    166
Sam Higgins  (9)    167
Conor Payne  (9)    167

## St Swithun Wells Catholic Primary School, Eastleigh
Gabrielle Tierling  (9)    168
Rebecca Platt  (8)    168
Rajan Rattan  (9)    168
Josephine Brennan Bavington  (9)    168
Matthew Dolbear  (8)    169
Jacque Harris  (9)    169
Craig Mellor  (9)    169
Danielle Coombs  (9)    169
Shannon Lima  (8)    170
Tyron Prentice  (9)    170

## Sharps Copse Primary School
Kayleigh Thompson  (9)    170
Alexandra King  (7)    170
Thomas Smith  (10)    171
Matthew Saunders  (10)    171
Kayleigh Roberts  (9)    171
Shaun Eckstein  (9)    172
Tristan Jobber  (9)    172
Mollie Parker  (9)    173
Jordan Goodwin  (9)    173
Alex MacDonald  (9)    174
Sarah Clarke  (9)    174
Ben Butt  (9)    174
Ellie-Mae Matthews  (9)    175

Zac Watson  (10)                                        175
Marley Palmer  (9)                                      175


**Tanners Brook Junior School**
Natasha Davis  (10)                                     176
Megan Cave  (9)                                         176
Kirstin McKinven  (10)                                  176
Natasha Grogan  (10)                                    177
Robin Moran  (9)                                        177
Dominic Ford  (10)                                      178
James Tilley  (9)                                       178
Luke Harris & Jack Lazarski  (10)                       179
Arjan Purewal  (9)                                      179
Rebecca Grogan  (10)                                    180
Greta Birch  (9)                                        180
Elisha Hawkins  (10)                                    181
Jack Weatherington  (10)                                181
Ali Hemy  (10)                                          181
Abigail James  (10)                                     182
Harpreet Kaur Potiwal  (9)                              182
Brandon Shephard  (9)                                   182
Harpage Kaur Bhakar  (10)                               183
Demi-Lea Grinsell  (10)                                 183
Kirstie Browning  (9)                                   183
Sophie Spicer  (9)                                      184
Amy Harmsworth  (10)                                    184
Kaylee White  (9)                                       185
Nathan Earley  (9)                                      185
Adam Kimber  (9)                                        186
Jessica Andrews  (8)                                    186
Elle Chivers  (10)                                      186
Sophie Adams  (9)                                       187
Jasvir Rathore  (9)                                     187
Michael Harmsworth  (7)                                 187
Ann-Marie Cummins  (8)                                  188
Max Richings  (8)                                       188
Liberty Reeves  (8)                                     188
Jack Sayers  (7)                                        189
Terri-Ann Ryder  (8)                                    189
Anna Godsell  (8)                                       189
Daisy Breed  (9)                                        190

| | |
|---|---:|
| Steve Mundy  (10) | 190 |
| Brooke Tomkins  (7) | 190 |
| Gemma Short  (9) | 191 |
| Kieran Joseph  (10) | 191 |
| Josh Attwood  (8) | 191 |
| Edward Sivyour  (10) | 192 |
| Rhea Waters  (10) | 192 |
| Lucy Smith  (7) | 192 |
| Liam Gale  (9) | 193 |
| Jack Evans  (8) | 193 |
| Connor Kenway  (7) | 193 |
| Munraj Purewal  (8) | 194 |
| Le'ana Montana  (7) | 194 |
| Veronica Tebano  (7) | 194 |
| Jack Gallacher  (8) | 195 |
| Megan Ashford-Hett  (7) | 195 |
| James Johnson  (7) | 195 |
| Mitchell Parker  (10) | 196 |
| Jessica Eves  (7) | 196 |
| Taylar Iason  (7) | 196 |
| Harry Smith  (9) | 197 |
| Nicole Roberts  (9) | 197 |
| Ashleigh Horeman  (7) | 197 |
| Ellis White  (10) | 198 |
| Jordan Hayball  (8) | 198 |
| Sean Neary  (7) | 198 |
| Kerry Cook  (7) | 199 |
| Bethany Holman  (9) | 199 |
| Chelsea Kenway  (8) | 199 |
| Michael Bolton  (7) | 199 |
| Chelsey-Lea Mouland  (7) | 200 |
| Victoria Lambert  (7) | 200 |
| Laura Challis  (7) | 200 |
| Molly Cole  (8) | 201 |
| Michael Hudson  (8) | 201 |
| Bradley Bennett  (8) | 201 |
| Tahnina Longman  (8) | 202 |
| Ellen Belcher  (7) | 202 |
| Charlie Maddocks  (7) | 202 |
| Courtney Skading  (7) | 203 |
| Tia Wassell  (8) | 203 |
| Sarah Toye  (7) | 203 |

## The Crescent Primary School

## The Grey House School

## Whiteley Primary School

## Whitewater CE Primary School

# The Poems

## The Magic Box

*(Based on 'Magic Box' by Kit Wright)*

I will put in my box . . .
The big, bright moon shining in the blue watery sea
And the reflection in the blue watery water.

My box is made from . . .
Hard, solid, strong birds
And metal that will never break.

I will put in my box . . .
Fishing food, luncheon meat, sweetcorn and bread
I will go over to America to go fishing.

**Caroll Barnes (10)**


## Trapped In Space

Space, an illuminous moon,
Space, with its glistening stars,
Don't worry, I'll be home soon,
Darling, I'm not very far.

Deep space, now I am dying,
I may never see you again,
You are so caring,
But I'm not your dragon's bane.

Space has trapped me in its grasp,
It's holding me tightly away,
I'm stuck in its tight clasp,
I'm in my eternal sleep.

**Revis Doherty (9)**
**Bramley CE Primary School**

# Sun

I'm dying,
I'm fading,
I'm weak and I'm pleading,
Praying for life and not for sorrow.

Joy in my heart will never be
Life is a joy that I will never see.

I'm boiling,
I'm sizzling,
Myself is cooking,
Spitting fire rocks as big as the moon.

Going to die, my ever fading light
I will never be so bright.

**Frances Robinson (10)**
**Bramley CE Primary School**


# Moonlight

The shimmery rays shine down on Earth.
Always remembering our star's birth.
The sun gives it light.
That's why it's bright.
Colder than deep blue ice.

**Nicola Bayley (9)**
**Bramley CE Primary School**


# Moon

The moon is miles and miles in outer space,
Reached only by the bravest astronauts,
Zoom goes the rocket, blazing with fire,
One small step for man, one big step for mankind!

**Sam Naylor (11)**
**Bramley CE Primary School**

# Martians Are Here

When I went to the moon,
You'll never guess what I saw,
I'll tell you what I saw,
I saw a Martian,
Yes, a Martian.
It was ugly and fat,
Had spots all over its face,
I didn't like it at all,
So I cried and went back to Earth.

**Gemma Withers  (11)**
**Bramley CE Primary School**


# A Frozen Still Moon

A cold shimmering night.
A zillion light years away.
A frozen still moon waits for the horizon to appear.
A rocket lands with flaming fires.
Swirling dust round and round.
Another night ahead
Just waiting, waiting.

**Olivia Barrett  (10)**
**Bramley CE Primary School**


# A Space Limerick

There was an alien from Mars,
Who didn't like the stars,
He got stuck on the moon,
And met the spoon,
And they drove away in a car!

**Jade Lander-Sims  (11)**
**Bramley CE Primary School**

# Space

J upiter was as red as the blood inside you
U ranus glistened in the reflection of the moon
P eople look up at the stars as if they were there
I mmediately after a rocket left, meteors would come
T omorrow the sun will rise on Earth but space will be dark
E arth is spinning slowly in the solar system
R acing through the sky go the meteors.

**Elly Willis  (9)**
**Bramley CE Primary School**


# Space

S tars flash in the night sky
P lanets go on forever
A steroids come flying down from space
C omets fly over us all shimmering in the night sky
E arth spins around and hopefully will live forever.

Space.

**Charlotte Ager  (10)**
**Bramley CE Primary School**


# Space

S un shining
P lanets whirling
A steroids whizzing
C raters resting
E arth rotating.

**Caroline Lowry-Whetton  (10)**
**Bramley CE Primary School**

## Space

S pace is like a dark nightmare that no one can escape from
P lanets are like overpowering bullies picking on all of the
little stars, dotted in the atmosphere
A stronauts feel weightless, and unprotected as they float around
in the unfamiliar universe
C harming stars, like droplets of shimmering paint
which have been dropped onto a black velvet blanket
E verlasting life which is still to be discovered.

**Joshua Harvey  (11)**
**Bramley CE Primary School**


## Meteor

M esmerizing showers of meteors
E ntertaining but deadly
T ogether they could spell disaster but
E verybody likes to watch them
O r they'll miss a very good experience
R eally brilliant, really cool.

**Matthew Smith  (10)**
**Bramley CE Primary School**


## Space

S aturn with the ear-piercing sound
P luto with the icy cold ground
A stronauts floating around
C omets with the speed
E arth with the greed.

**Thomas Stevens  (10)**
**Bramley CE Primary School**

# Wild Space

I set off in my spaceship,
Up to a world above,
Suddenly my ship did a flip,
And I fell in love.

The planets were spinning,
Like a merry-go-round,
The stars were madly glistening,
And a shooting star I found.

I leapt out of my ride,
This big sun burning ahead,
All of a sudden there was an alien by my side,
And it had a big green head.

**Rosie York  (9)**
**Bramley CE Primary School**


# Rockets In Space

Rockets plummeting up to the sky,
Landing on planets way up high,
Seeing debris floating by,
Shimmering, shooting stars floating
Around in the midnight sky.

Space, was I actually here or was it a dream?
Spotting my home planet Earth.
So many million miles away,
It didn't seem real but it was,
It wasn't a dream.

**Megan Moody  (11)**
**Bramley CE Primary School**

# Space

Preparing for take-off,
The pressure is rising.

The countdown begins
It's mesmerizing.

Travelling through the atmosphere,
To an unknown world.
A sky of midnight black you see,
Arrogant meteors being hurled.

The stars are pinpricks in the sky,
Planets orbit the sun,
Watch out for an alien,
With a laser gun.

Shooting stars fly across the sky,
With immense impact.
The sun has scary solar storms,
And hey, that's a fact.

**Bianca Rodriguez (10)**
**Bramley CE Primary School**


# Blast-Off

A rocket, waiting to go into outer space
First load the fuel
Then put in the provisions,
In go the astronauts ready for the adventure of a lifetime,
Off to Mars.
Start the engine, 5, 4, 3, 2, 1, 0
We have permission to take-off
5, 4, 3, 2, 1
*Blast-off.*

**Zosia Hermaszewska (10)**
**Bramley CE Primary School**

# It's A Small World

Planets chase around the sun,
Smiling, having fun.
Stars skip round and round,
In circles, they sing with no sound.

Saturn's playing hula hoop,
I say, he's gathered quite a troop.
He's been hooping for centuries,
So we begged him to share, please, please, please.

Black hole wants some friends,
So he sucks things in and pretends,
To blend in with the blue,
So watch out, *You!*

Pluto barks at Mickey Mouse,
Then he sees a starry louse.
He broke off the orbit of sun,
So soon he broke into a run.

Meteor crashes through the world,
While in sleep, people are curled.
He hits Atmosphere so she weeps,
As his fiery blackness he keeps.

**Stephanie Alsop (10)**
**Bramley CE Primary School**


# Feelings Of Space

Space smells like eternal death creeping up on you
Space sounds like an ear-piercing silence
Space tastes like freedom that will be snatched from you
Space feels like loneliness and hatred
Space looks like a black abyss with distant stars
Shedding their light upon you
Feelings are important in space,
They are your only friend in the deep dark wilderness.

**Stephen Brownstone (11)**
**Bramley CE Primary School**

# The Solar System

All the planets stand in a line,
The sun, the moon and all the nine,
They rotate spinning around the sun,
Their million laps never done.

Pluto's the furthest planet away,
Colder and colder, so they say.
Mercury's at the opposite end,
Different shades of blue – a new fashion trend.

The moon is the famous rocky ball,
That circles the Earth, he'll never fall.
Whilst the sun is burning, she's a fiery star,
She stays in one place and doesn't move very far.

This is all you need to know about the planets and the moon,
I'll bet you anything that we'll see you very soon.
So it's goodbye from the sun and all the nine,
Go back to Earth, it's about time!

**Amy Stringer  (10)**
**Bramley CE Primary School**


# Are There Martians In Space?

When I was walking home from school,
It started to pour down with rain,
I wondered what was happening up there,
Were the Martians playing a game?

Yes, the Martians, the Martians,
I wonder who they are?
I wonder if I could meet one soon,
And then I would be a star!

**Jordan Jackson  (10)**
**Bramley CE Primary School**

# First Man On The Moon

Suddenly taking off high
Soaring and bounding through the sky
Further and further into space
Trying to stay with the beeping trace
No one knows how long it will take
As the rocket starts to break and flake
The shadows of the moon are in sight
But to get there the space rocket will have to fight
Closer and closer they get to the moon
The astronauts hoping to arrive very soon
As they land on the moon normally seen in the sky
They jump for joy, right up high.

*They have done it*
*The first people to land on the moon.*

**Hannah Skelton (11)**
**Bramley CE Primary School**


# Pluto

Sadly drifting round and round,
The sun holding me in the celestial dance
Cold, so very cold
Slowly slipping into the cold depths of the
Universe.
So very lonely am I,
I watch the moon being explored every other month,
Even Mars has probes sent to its red dust of
Wonder.
*I am unloved by all!*

**Sam Cooper (11)**
**Bramley CE Primary School**

# An Alien Limerick

There was
An alien from Mars,
Who liked to eat the stars.
One got stuck in his throat
And he started to choke
So decided to eat
Choccy bars.

**Rachel Francis  (11)**
**Bramley CE Primary School**


# Space

Planets, comets all live in space
I can see the man in the moon's face.

Boiling, flaming, how hot is the sun?
It is more than a million times bigger than Earth.

Mars, Pluto, I've seen them all,
I've even seen the Milky Way.

I'm going back home, to where I was born,
Where I live, it is now dawn.

**Charlotte Draper  (9)**
**Bramley CE Primary School**


# Saturn

Saturn is very cold.
The ring around is ice and stone.
Saturn is made of gas.
A space probe trying to land.
Saturn is orange and yellow.
I like Saturn best of all.
Do you?

**Katie King  (9)**
**Bramley CE Primary School**

# Space

U nderstanding the universe may be very hard
N othing in space would you see in your backyard
I nside all the planets it would be very hot
V arieties are massive if you want to see a lot
E verything you see out there is very far away
R ockets could take you there if you agree to pay
S atellites are useful if you want to talk to me
E normous things in space are a wonderful sight to see.

G reat big stars float around in galaxies
A steroids fly around so everybody sees
L ight would be quite useful for it's so dark
A stronauts jump around as if it is a park
X ylophones you couldn't hear cos sound can't travel through,
Y ears it would take to get out of our planet zoo.

**Jamie Baird (10)**
**Bramley CE Primary School**


# Moonlight Orbiting

S tars shimmering all night long
P eople begin to hear a noise from doors shutting
A shooting star shoots across the sky, shimmering
C ome and see the wonders of the world
E veryone comes to see the universe
W atching the planets zoom past
A planet looking lonely in the sky
T o the middle of the sky shoots a rocket
C ome and see the wonders of the world
H ill hollows in the sky.

**Mia Sung (9)**
**Bramley CE Primary School**

# Universe

U p, up and away
N eptune, Pluto, Mercury and Mars
I 've seen them all
V enturing through space
E arth so far away
R oaming from planet to planet
S peeding through hyperspace
E xiting space, entering Earth; home at last!

**Declan Mattingley (10)**
**Bramley CE Primary School**


# Space

S tars like ever glowing fireflies leading the way to
   discoveries unknown
P robes helping us to discover and learn
A stronauts in rockets going where no man has been before
C rescent moon giving night light to the world
E ver glowing, heat producing sun, glistening in the sky
   like a giant diamond.

**Emma Capel (11)**
**Bramley CE Primary School**


# Space

S pace is like an endless corridor
P ainted with black all around you.
A ll the planets glistening like golden jewellery.
C old sucking out all your happiness,
E mptiness all around you.

**Alex Davies (9)**
**Bramley CE Primary School**

# Asteroids

A steroids everywhere dart
S illy rockets pull apart
T he astronauts go up to space
E arth is the planet that is ace
R ockets return to the human race
O range shaped sun burning with fun
I nteresting sun helps Earth run
D istant planets waiting to unfold
S un is a star we have been told.

**Liam Torrie (10)**
**Bramley CE Primary School**


# In Space

S hooting stars twinkling in the dark, immense sky
P lummeting meteors zooming by
A liens living on the scorching sun
C ould they shoot you with their laser guns?
E verywhere an amazing spectacle to see, in space!

**Katie Player (10)**
**Bramley CE Primary School**


# Space

S pace is an endless void of blackness
P owerful beyond compare
A ll things happen here
C hilling to the bone, no one out there
E mptiness like nothing else . . .

**James Caldwell (11)**
**Bramley CE Primary School**

# The Universe

U nknown galaxies never to be told
N obody leaving gravity's hold
I magine rockets being pulled apart
V anishing pieces everywhere dart
E arth being hit by a solar flare
R espiration needs air
S putnik entering hyperspace
E arth is the only place for the human race.

**Charlie Goddard  (9)**
**Bramley CE Primary School**

# Space

S pace, a dark and wonderful place
P lace where people see the past
A ll the stars shining down on you
C onstellations all over the sky
E ach and every planet orbiting each other.

**William Read  (10)**
**Bramley CE Primary School**

# Space

S tars in the moonlight
P assing the black hole, dying with their might
A liens with their three eyes
C omets and satellites passing, winking at night
E arth is after Venus, but before Mars.

**Ben Giles  (10)**
**Bramley CE Primary School**

# Nine Planets In A Row

Dark and black, an empty space,
Aliens roam of a different race,
Planets circle the sun, air lord,
Attached together with invisible cord.

Small Mercury not far from the sun,
Molten rock begins to run,
Venus is not far from us,
No one gives it a lot of fuss.

The most important of them all,
Earth is splattered with a big whirlpool.
Mars is next, the planet red,
Rover made it, the other fled.

Jupiter with its big red spot,
Red is spilling from a gunshot.
Now Saturn's turn with its rings,
Shot out of the big bang with a ping.

Uranus now, we're getting smaller,
A big blue planet but not any taller,
Neptune is the second to last,
Formed by a rock, it lives in the past.

Pluto is the last in the row,
But it might grow, you never know.

**Megan Fright  (10)**
**Bramley CE Primary School**


# There Was An Old Cook From Mars

There was an old cook from Mars
Who made shiny cakes from the stars
She flew to the moon
On her big wooden spoon
That loopy old cook from Mars.

**Alice Henderson  (10)**
**Bramley CE Primary School**

## Shimmering Stars

S tars shimmer in the midnight sky
P ieces scattered in air around us
A stronauts floating on the moon
C omets shooting through the air
E veryone watching, all is near.

W aiting, watching don't know what's going to appear
A fter seeing absolutely nothing there
T orching Earth we are almost there
C ome and see the wonders of the world
H illy rocks, we're almost there.

**Danielle Wood  (8)**
**Bramley CE Primary School**


## Space

S pace is lonely, no one's there
P eople are on Earth where oxygen is in the air
A liens may be lurking on Uranus or Saturn
'C ause even if they are, does it really matter?
E ven right now they may be seeing, how to get rid
   of every human being!

**Richard Park  (10)**
**Bramley CE Primary School**


## Space

S tars shooting
P lanets orbiting
A stronauts gliding
C omets darting
E arth circling the sun.

**Connor Stewart  (10)**
**Bramley CE Primary School**

# The Shimmering Moon

A cold sphere.
A shimmering night.
A billion, light years away.
Stood there all night until the break of dawn.
Swirling dust as the sun appears.
The grey-white moon disappears.
But still we know it lingers near.

**Amy Berntsen (10)**
**Bramley CE Primary School**


# Space Limerick

A young man went into space,
He thought it an unusual place,
He landed on Mars,
Saw lots of stars,
And met an unusual race.

**Francis Dredge-Hetherington (11)**
**Bramley CE Primary School**


# Earth

Rotation, rotation, it's rotating right now.
Every moment I wonder how.
Gravity, gravity pulls us to the core.
You can't get out there, it's pulling more.

**Connor McCallum (10)**
**Bramley CE Primary School**

# Vikings!

Here they come!
The Vikings!
Some are tall,
Some are cruel.

They are armed with weapons
Shiny and silver
Swords and spears, I am drowning in tears
Coming straight from my fears.

They will invade our country
Tear the people
Limb from limb
What am I going to do
With all this din?

**Michaela Andrews  (8)**
**Castle Hill Junior School**


# Vikings!

Here they come!
Vikings with sharp swords like claws.
Here they come,
With flames on their sticks.
Here they come,
Shaking their flaming hot fire
To burn down the city to the ground!
Thatched roofs burned down,
Doors fallen down like burglars,
Knocking down doors.
*Here they come!*
*Aarghhhh!*

**Liberty Barrett  (9)**
**Castle Hill Junior School**

# Vikings!

Here comes the Vikings!
The frightening golden dragon head glints
In the mist,
As they come nearer and nearer,
They are
Looking at me as
I stare
In horror.
I must shout a warning.

**Chloe Lacy  (8)**
**Castle Hill Junior School**


# Vikings!

Here they come with flaming torches
Here they come with shining swords
Here they come with sharp, sharp axes
Here they come with glistening helmets
Here they come, they're frightening
Here they come, hide!

**Jade-Marie Hide  (9)**
**Castle Hill Junior School**


# Vikings!

Here they come with deadly axes
Here they come with terrifying shields
Here they come with sharp words
Here they come with flaming torches
Here they come with dangerous helmets
Here they come, the *Vikings!*

**Nathan Oliver  (9)**
**Castle Hill Junior School**

## Vikings!

The Vikings charged in like a stampede.
Suddenly *Boom!*
The door went flat on the floor
Shall I fight, or shall I not?
There is no time to lose
Yes I will fight although I'm a woman,
Who said women can't fight?
Anyway I feel petrified.
Aarghh!
Suddenly the room goes silent.
What have I done?
What shall I do?

**Natasha Hudson  (8)**
**Castle Hill Junior School**


## Vikings!

Fire is a sign of their power
Dragons show their bravery
Swords and shields show their might
An invincible army of warriors
We have no chance of survival.

**Carl Gardiner  (8)**
**Castle Hill Junior School**


## Vikings!

Down by the shore a big boat lies
While really big men come walking by
They're big and tough, and smelly too
I wonder who's the leader of this vicious crew.

**Corran Kingsbury  (9)**
**Castle Hill Junior School**

# Vikings!

Here they come, the scary mean old Vikings!
    Here they come with big brown dragon boats
        Here they come, some say they're traders
          Some say they're invaders.
      I am very scared. *Bang!*

They're here now with big black torches,
Their long thin swords and their large gold helmets.

      Help! Here they are!

**Olivia Willis  (8)**
**Castle Hill Junior School**


# Vikings!

The big dragon head is moving in the water.
Those Vikings can see me and they think I'm scared, but I'm not!
I'd better fold my tent up and get ready to go back home.

The Vikings are coming towards me!
I'd better hide my treasure quick.
Me and Teddy will run back home.
The big golden dragon head on their boat won't scare me,
But it might scare Teddy!

**Naomi Jones  (8)**
**Castle Hill Junior School**


# Vikings!

Who are the Vikings?
Where did they come from?
Did they trade things?
Do they use bombs?
I really wonder who the Vikings really are.
Will I ever know?

**Samuel Genovese  (9)**
**Castle Hill Junior School**

# Vikings!

The Vikings
Attacked furiously like cheetahs pouncing on their prey.
The Vikings
Had vicious dragon heads on their boats that glistened in the
distance.

The Vikings
Had bright shields protecting the bloodthirsty invaders.
The Vikings
Terrified the Anglo-Saxons.
The Vikings
Succeeded in their invasion.

**Vashist Motkur (9)**
**Castle Hill Junior School**

# Vikings!

Here the Vikings come!
Here they come
With their lit torches
Here they come
With their dangerous weapons
Here they come
I don't think I can take it anymore.

**Sydney White (9)**
**Castle Hill Junior School**

# Vikings!

When the Vikings came striking,
Running like a bull,
The monks did not let them rule.
As the monastery went down in flames,
The fierce old Vikings went 'Hooray, Hooray!'

**Jacob Brown (9)**
**Castle Hill Junior School**

# Vikings!

I can see a golden dragon head in the mist
It is coming closer and closer
What will happen to me?
I feel terrified!
They're jumping out of the boat!
They're running towards our village
Help!
Be afraid
Very afraid!

**Beverley Stainer  (9)**
Castle Hill Junior School


# Vikings!

Oh no, here come the Vikings,
In their big longboat!
The golden head looks scary
When it is afloat!

Here come the Vikings
With their great swords and shields!
They are coming to invade
As they charge across the fields!

**Patrik Toobe  (9)**
Castle Hill Junior School


# Vikings!

Here they come with their torches lit.
Here they come with their swords waving.
Here they come with their coloured shields.
We bury our treasure,
But they soon find it.
We run
And we never come back.

**Wade Vince  (9)**
Castle Hill Junior School

# Vikings!

When the Vikings came, they came
They came in their ships, their ships.
They look frightening, very frightening.

They burned our village, our village
They killed our people, our people.
They knocked down our church, our holy church.

They stole our treasure, our treasure,
I lost my home, my home,
My mum and dad died, they died.

Now it is morning, it's morning
I am lonely, very lonely.
Now I walk alone, alone.

**Lori-Ann Wyatt  (8)**
**Castle Hill Junior School**


# Vikings Are Coming

They come towards me!
The Vikings
They've come to steal our treasure
The Vikings know we have some
They want it all
I must run to save my life
I go to the door with my teddy
I see the golden head
I'm not scared of them
But I am sure Teddy is!

**Lauren Ludlow  (9)**
**Castle Hill Junior School**

# Vikings!

Here come the Vikings!
I need to take my dog
Here come the Vikings!
I need to hide
Here come the Vikings!
Where can I hide?
I better hide in the kitchen
Here come the Vikings!
They're coming to the kitchen
Here come the Vikings!
Aarghhh!

**Sam Fettin  (8)**
Castle Hill Junior School


# Vikings!

The Vikings!
Come and charge away.
They creep like
Mice in the hay.
They want the treasure
With a lot of pleasure
And fight and fight and fight away.

**Charlie Hannah  (9)**
Castle Hill Junior School


# What Is Young?

As young as spring at the start
Of the new year,
As young as a tiny, newborn baby,
As young as a recently made web,
And as young as fresh prints in the snow.

**Suzi Goose  (11)**
Cove Junior School

# Camels

The caramel camel
Travels calmly
Through the desert
For days on end.

The cinnamon camel
Stores food
Like a gerbil
In its hump.

The coffee camel
Moves like
A ship
In the desert.

The chocolate-coloured camel
Spits like a
Chelsea football player.

**Charlie Long  (11)**
Cove Junior School


# Tarantula

There's a tarantula
Up on the wall
On the window
On the stall.

There's a tarantula
Here and there
There's a tarantula
That goes
*Anywhere!*
There's a tarantula
Which has eight eyes
There's a tarantula
Which likes maggot pies.

**Andrew Dyos  (9)**
Cove Junior School

# When I Am Old . . .

When I am old,
I will go to far-off places
And I will dance with the
Famous Elton John.

When I am old
I will go to town
To buy pink furry thongs
So I can look gorgeous.

When I am old
I will eat what I want
And I will be
The world's best chocolate eater.

When I am old
I will travel round on a sonic scooter
And I will be the coolest
Granny in the world.

**Caris Brooks  (10)**
**Cove Junior School**


# The Crab

The stripy,
Dark orange crab
Is camouflaged
By a flow
Of sands.
The magnificent crab
Is strolling
With its titanium
Claws!

**Marcus Gale  (10)**
**Cove Junior School**

# What Is Angry?

As angry as a ferocious ox at feeding time!

As angry as a miner who left his gold
In a mine!

As angry as Santa who forgot to
Deliver his toys!

As angry as a teacher who is
Bellowing at some boys!

As angry as a mother who has lost
Her baby!

As angry as when a war was lost by
The navy!

As angry as a skater, who fell off his
Skateboard!

As angry as a warrior who got
Stabbed with a sword!

As angry as some aliens who have no
Ships!

As angry as a fish and chip shop
Which has run out of chips!

As angry as an historian who has
Broken his artefact!

As angry as a sculptor whose
Sculpture got cracked!

As angry as a farmer who has lost his
Sheep!

As angry as a swimmer who can't
Swim in the deep!

**Ryan Cook (11)**
**Cove Junior School**

# What Is In The Box?

What is in the box
Is it . . .

A glittering gold fairy
        Gliding
An emerald green pixie
        Zooming
A sparkling silver grasshopper,
        Hopping
A fluorescent pink butterfly,
        Fluttering
A shimmering turquoise dragonfly,
        Floating
A static orange fly,
        Dashing.
We don't know
        Let's look!

**Paige Gibbons (9)**
Cove Junior School

# What Is Powerful?

As powerful as a mighty hurricane
Tearing down the rooftops,

As powerful as a fierce warrior fighting
Against a vicious lion,

As powerful as a tidal wave ripping out
Trees from land,

As powerful as a person's brain figuring
Out a maths question,

As powerful as a wise Egyptian God
Ruling the Egyptian slaves.

**Alexandra Davis (11)**
Cove Junior School

# What Is Cool?

As cool as a frosty lemonade
Ice cube!

As cool as a rebel motorbike
Dude!

As cool as the crisp air on a
Pine mountain top!

As cool as a yummy,
Refreshing jug of pop!

As cool as a racing car
Travelling 180mph!

As cool as a 1000 bags of
Sweets, all extra sour!

As cool as a bungee jumper,
All brave and wild!

As cool as a curry all hot –
Not mild!

As cool as not working,
Watching TV and being a slob.

As cool as an ice cream tester,
Now that's my dream job!

**Michael Salter  (11)**
**Cove Junior School**


# What Is Loud?

As loud as a shouting, pink mohican.
As loud as scared, screaming children,
Lost in a huge park.
As loud as the last heartbeat in a deserted room.
As loud as an abandoned baby's teardrop . . .
                    Falling.

**Emily Regan  (10)**
**Cove Junior School**

# What Is Angry?

As angry as a crocodile snapping at its prey.
As angry as an elephant, stomping with a stampede.
As angry as a piranha at feeding time.

As angry as the wind lashing through the trees.
As angry as the thunder clashing with the lightning.
As angry as a tornado whipping through the rooftops.

As angry as a bully goading his victim.
As angry as a hunter when the deer runs away.
As angry as a warrior when the battle is lost.

**Laura Pammer (11)**
Cove Junior School

# What Is Sharp?

As sharp as the taste of bitter lemon slipping down your throat.
As sharp as the point on a shiny needle piercing your smooth skin.
As sharp as the thrashing rain stinging your face.
As sharp as the feeling of dread creeping up your spine.
As sharp as the spine-chilling howl of a wolf.
As sharp as a pounding headache making you cringe in agony.
As sharp as a fox' s hearing in the crisp air of the dead of the night.

**Ailsa Winter (10)**
Cove Junior School

# What Is Rough?

As rough as a bumpy abrupt road made of gravel,
As rough as your extremely long-life journey,
As rough as the bottom of a bottle lid,
As you run your finger along it,
As rough as the Lincoln green carpet.

**Ryan Walters (10)**
Cove Junior School

# Books

I know a place,
Where all can go,
Lands of adventure,
Let your imagination flow,

I know a place,
Where many battles are fought,
Where cattle graze in the field,
Or where pirates sail again.

I know a place,
Where monsters live,
And you are the hero,
Or fly high in the sky.

I know a place,
Where all can go,
Lands of adventure,
Let your imagination flow.

**Hayden Orriss  (10)**
**Cove Junior School**

# What Is Evil?

As evil as a bully, menacing a victim,
As evil as a hunter, killing a stag,
As evil as a vampire, with a stone heart,
As evil as a ghoul, departed from this world.

As evil as a scientist, experimenting on animals,
As evil as a wolf, with slobbering fangs,
As evil as a jackal, baying to the moon,
As evil as a knife, piercing a heart.

As evil as war, death and destruction,
As evil as Hell, ragged and fiery,
As evil as a time bomb, about to explode,
As evil as an ogre, feasting on bones.

**Matthew Casey & Jamie Dawkins  (11)**
**Cove Junior School**

# Books

Books are fun
They take you places
Some are hilarious
With funny faces.

Some take you to the past
Some keep you in the present
Some take you to the future
Some take you up to Heaven.

Books are fun
They take you places
Some are hilarious
With funny faces.

Climbing up Jack's beanstalk
To the giant's lair
Inviting Goldilocks
And the three bears.

Books are fun
They take you places
Some are hilarious
With funny faces.

**Sophie Eynon (11)**
**Cove Junior School**

# Books

I know a secret door
Into a thousand amazing places
Willy Wonker's chocolate factory
Where you can eat some sweet laces.

A time machine that takes me
To ride the candy train
We can visit the Lake of Sunshine
And down the long lost lane.

I can visit the future
And even the past,
You can come with me
We'll reach Neverland at last.

We can visit Humpty Dumpty
We can climb his falling wall
We can climb Jack's Beanstalk
It's exceptionally tall.

I have quite amazing times
When I sit and read a book,
Find a comfy armchair
Turn the pages and look.

**Chloe Gray (10)**
**Cove Junior School**

# Ghosts

Ghosts today aren't spooky
They don't haunt people at night
It always happens in the daytime
Their midday delight.

Ghosts eat chicken stew
When it's warm and nice
They never eat spider cobwebs
(They're always as cold as ice)

They keep their howls in shape
They never let them crack
'Cos when they hit the high-notes
They sometimes go all slack.

Ghosts never go all dull
They always keep their white
But because they're not in shock
It's not all down to fright.

You'll see them walking down the street
So give them a cheery wave
But because they're ghosts today
They've got a soul to save.

**Chloë Rogers  (9)**
**Cove Junior School**


# What Is Deep?

As deep as the dank depths of the mighty ocean.
As deep as the dingy well of an unused dungeon.
As deep as an everlasting abyss.
As deep as a winding passage in a grimy gold mine.
As deep as the rotting roots of an ancient oak tree.
As deep as the red-hot core of the Earth.
As deep as the complicated tunnels of a mother mole.
As deep as a vine covered valley between two
                              snow-capped mountains.

**Lucy Irving  (10)**
**Cove Junior School**

# Books

A book can lead you anywhere
From China to the USA,
You could go absolutely anywhere
And you won't even have to pay.

Walking through a tunnel,
Looking all around,
It's a scary place
Deep underground.

You can march with some captains,
There would only be ten;
You could slay all the monsters
And cruel, evil men.

You could fly almost anywhere
Just like a sparrow,
Or learn from Robin Hood,
How to use a bow and arrow.

You could be a super hero,
Wandering round a grave,
Searching for Count Dracula
You must be exceptionally brave.

**Ryan Hughes  (10)**
**Cove Junior School**


# What Is Smooth?

As smooth as a slithery bar of soap sliding
Through my fingers.

As smooth as brand new lenses on my glasses
Glistening in the sun.

As smooth as a silk shirt on my shoulders.

As smooth as a sheet of shiny white paper,
Just newly printed.

As smooth as a newly buffed table in my living room.

**William Campos  (11)**
**Cove Junior School**

# Books

A book is a magical place
Where you can go deep in the jungle
Where you can swing and climb the trees
And be trapped in a bundle!

Go skipping through the woods
Taking brownies to Gran,
Or even fighting Hercules,
The biggest and strongest man!

Go to the forest,
Then meet with ET
Travel to his planet,
Just him and me!

When you open a book,
You feel great inside,
But you can meet the evil Chucky,
Then be scared by his bride!

It's where you eat a bowl of porridge,
But not the baby bears,
Climb into their tiny beds,
Then breaking all their chairs!

Meet a cheeky monkey,
Then chase him through the trees,
Or meet Winnie the Pooh,
Taking honey from the bees!

**Jasmine Blair (11)**
Cove Junior School

# What Is Hollow?

As hollow as an enormous Easter egg encased in a shiny silvery silk.
As hollow as a rotten tree trunk decaying and disintegrating.
As hollow as a dark box inside a spooky corner.
As hollow as a room once everyone has gone home.

**Sophie Lynch (10)**
Cove Junior School

# Books

Books can take you to faraway places,
To a wonderland and Neverland,
You can meet Alice and Peter Pan,
You can fight Captain Hook and hope you will not die.

Books will transport you underwater,
To dive with dangerous fish,
You could meet Ariel the mermaid,
And all her underwater world.

Books can swipe you away,
To the top of a pyramid,
Or hidden with the mummies,
In a hidden underground tomb.

Books can hypnotize you,
Or put you in a trance,
You'll wake up from your magical world,
Already late for dinner.

**James Lalor (11)**
**Cove Junior School**

# Teachers Today

Teachers fat
Teachers thin
They all deserve
To live in a bin.

They don't let you out
They keep you in all day
They don't have any fun in them
They treat you like a slave.

They keep an eye on you
You can't get away
That is why
No one likes to stay.

**Anna Stevens (9)**
**Cove Junior School**

# Books

A book is a place
Where you can go
Whenever you wish
Just open it up
And step in.

Walking through a magic forest
Looking for Robin Hood
Sailing the seven seas
Searching for Captain Hook.

Creeping round a giant castle
Hunting for Frankenstein
Looking over every wall
Searching for Humpty Dumpty.

Searching through a labyrinth

Looking for a Minotaur
Looking on Mount Olympus
For the Greek god Zeus.

A book is a place
Where you can go
Whenever you wish
Just open it up
And step in.

**Mark Haffenden  (9)**
**Cove Junior School**

# Books

Open a book and step inside,
Towards a magical world,
Full of surprise.

I can fly up high to the stars,
Meet the cow who jumped over the moon,
Bump into an alien's spaceship,
And land not a moment too soon.

I can explore the spooky castle,
With the help of the Famous Five,
To try and catch Captain Hook,
Whilst he takes me by surprise.

I can slay the golden dragon,
With Excalibur itself,
Whilst having tea with Cinderella,
And lunch with a naughty elf.

I can meet the evil Olaf,
And the delightful Alice,
Go to the ball with Cinderella,
In the handsome prince's palace.

Open a book and step inside,
Towards a magical world,
Full of surprise.

**Emily Sanders (11)**
**Cove Junior School**

# I Love To Read

I love to read – it's such a special thing to do.
There are books full with magic and wands,
Sad things and happy things,
All you need is a key to open the door.

I love to read – it's such a special thing to do.
You can find out about first aid or maybe even slugs,
Recipes for chocolate crisp cakes and lemon meringue,
All you need is a key to open the door.

I love to read – it's such a special thing to do.
You can go to the underwater world,
Or maybe even Hell,
All you need is a key to open the door.

I love to read – it's such a special thing to do.
There are books full with magic and wands,
Sad things and happy things,
All you need is a key to open the door.

I love to read – it's such a special thing to do.

**Leanne Beales (10)**
**Cove Junior School**


# Books

I know a secret door
Into a world of stories
Tales of battles won and lost
Bloody defeats and glories.

Meet Jack and Hill, Legolas and Aragorn,
Peter Piper, Captain Hook and Peter Pan
Spider-Man, Superman or Gandalf
All you have to do is sit down and read a book.

I know a secret door
Into a world of stories
Tales of battles won and lost
Bloody defeats and glories.

**Joshua Bouette (10)**
**Cove Junior School**

# A Book Is A Place

I know a secret passageway
That leads to extraordinary places,
Where there are bloodsucking vampires
And people with two faces.

I'm running from a bone-crushing bear
I'm hiding in a cave,
Now I'm travelling back in the past
Way back to the stone age.

You can meet Captain Hook
In battle with Peter Pan,
Maybe if you're lucky
You could fly with Superman.

I know a secret passageway
That leads to extraordinary places
You'll visit a world of make-believe
Meet people of different races.

**Matthew Webster  (11)**
**Cove Junior School**

# What Teachers Do?

Teachers today are not very good,
They always are a pain
When they eat their dinner,
They make a dirty stain.

Up in the staffroom
Which stinks of herbal tea?
They sometimes spill the kettle
This leads to a burnt knee.

Teachers come to school looking in a mess
With their bright yellow shoes
They are leaving luminous trails,
So we can see the clues.

**Kimberley Maunders  (9)**
**Cove Junior School**

# Books

A book is a place
Where you can go
Whenever you wish
Just open it up
And step in!

Searching through a toy chest
Looking for Woody himself
Walking through a dark maze
Searching for a Minotaur

Seeing Stig of the dump
In his den on the hill
Bumping into the three little pigs
Or even Jack or Jill

Creeping up a giant beanstalk
Or even meeting Red Riding Hood
You might see Captain Hook
In a big sea of blood.

A book is a place
Where you can go
Open it up
And step in!

**Alex Schofield  (9)**
**Cove Junior School**


# Secret Agents

Secret agents are taken in easily
And always getting it wrong
Falling in love with the wrong girl
Cos she's wearing a pink, furry thong.

Secret agents today are silly,
And always get it wrong
They aren't very conscientious
They drive their boss into song.

**Michael Whicker  (11)**
**Cove Junior School**

# Books

A book is like a pathway
Leading anywhere you wish,
From a beautiful mermaid
To a thousand minute fish.

You may think I'm just sitting
When really in my head,
I'm solving a murder mystery
Before I go to bed.

I'm sprinting like a cheetah
Or soaring like a bird,
I'm swimming like a fish
Even though it sounds absurd!

It takes me back in time,
To a time when knights were brave;
And sometimes even further
To when people lived in caves.

They fling me to the future,
To planets far away;
They lead me to adventures
Lasting April until May.

I meet monsters and dragons
Harry Potter and Captain Hook,
Good guys and bad ones,
When I sit and read a book.

A book is like a pathway
Leading anywhere you wish,
From a beautiful mermaid
To a thousand minute fish.

**Ryan Collingham (11)**
**Cove Junior School**

# Books

A book is a place,
Where you can live,
It's an adventure,
A place to give!

A book is a place,
Where you can fly
For miles and miles,
In a clear blue sky!

A book is a place,
To get in the motion,
In the sun,
Or maybe the ocean!

A book is a place,
Where nothing suffers,
A book is amazing,
Like no others!

A book is a place,
Where you can live,
It's an adventure,
A place to give.

**Rosie Chambers (11)**
**Cove Junior School**


# What Is Soft?

As soft as a fragile, faint feather
As soft as a gentle, calm breeze,
As soft as a human's pale skin,
As soft as a creamy, pale ice cream,
As soft as a sweet bird's voice,
As soft as a fluffy kitten's fur.

**Emily Coxhead (11)**
**Cove Junior School**

# A Book Is A Place

I know a secret key
To take you to terrifying places,
Where dead people walk
With their evil hideous faces.

I could be Cinderella
Going to the ball
Meeting Alice in Wonderland
Skipping down the hall.

I'm chasing after a robber
Who's incredibly fast,
He jumps through a portal
Which takes him to the past.

I'm a super hero
Flying through the sky
Or even a super villain
Who's very slick and sly.

I could be Gandalf
With mystic, hidden powers
Trying to eliminate
The dreaded Two Towers.

**Joe Hardy (11)**
**Cove Junior School**


# What Is Deep?

As deep as a powerful machine can dig,
As deep as you think when you write a poem,
As deep as a worm tunnelling underground,
As deep as anger when you blow,
As deep as an ancient pot goes,
As deep as space will ever end,
As deep as the deep blue sea.

**Kudzai Sitima (9)**
**Cove Junior School**

# Books

I know a place where there's nothing I can't do
So I can fly like Superman or ride on silver snakes
But everyone thinks I'm sitting on a chair.

You can visit scary places and meet Captain Hook,
But this can only happen . . .
If you sit and read a book!

I know a place where there's nothing I can't do
I can be on top of the world
I can do whatever you want
And no one can say 'That's impossible!'

I know a world where there's nothing
I can't do . . .
I can fly like Superman.

**Jack Hoggard  (9)**
**Cove Junior School**


# Snails

Five little snails went to climb up the door
One went too slow, so that left four.
Four little snails went to play with a bee
One got stung, so that left three.
Three little snails went to play a tune,
One got a headache, so that left two.
Two little snails went to have fun
One got stuck, so that left one.
One little snail went to look for a bun,
Got crushed by a human, so that left none.

**Ashley Noyce  (9)**
**Marchwood Junior School**

# An Elephant

An elephant has . . .
Eyes like tiny flies popping out of plants
Legs like bendy banana trees swaying in the breeze
Ears like tall icy mountains standing high in the sky
A trunk like a scaly, long snake hanging from a bush
A memory like a stone-age grandad, cooking at a fire.

An elephant is . . .
As wrinkled as a strawberry lollipop sticking to some paper
As stately as an important royal queen walking through a
                                    crowd of people
As slow as two lively snails sliding down the wall
As heavy as a gigantic village covering lots of ground
As strong as the strongest wrestler practising with weights.

**Carissa Bowen (9)**
**Marchwood Junior School**


# An Elephant

An elephant has . . .
Eyes like small grapes in the sunshine
Legs like giant towers in New York
Ears like small bits of paper to be used
A trunk like a bendy banana in a big field
A memory like a clever robot working in a factory.

An elephant is . . .
As wrinkled as an old-age pensioner walking around
As stately as a red car without a steering wheel on the road
As slow as a slimy snail going down the road
As heavy as a big plane getting ready to take-off
As strong as a ginormous monster coming out to get you.

**Jordie Scott (9)**
**Marchwood Junior School**

# Snakes

Five brown snakes went to roar
One got detention, so that left four.

Four brown snakes went to catch a bee
One got stung, so that left three.

Three brown snakes went for goo
One got stuck, so that left two.

Two brown snakes went to have fun
One got caught, so that left one.

One brown snake went for a bun,
Got too fat and that left none.

**Matthew Hill  (9)**
**Marchwood Junior School**


# Five Black Dogs

Five black dogs went to the door
One fell over, so that left four.

Four black dogs went up a tree
One tripped up, so that left three.

Three black dogs went to the zoo
One was eaten, so that left two.

Two black dogs went for the gun
One got shot, so that left one.

One black dog went for a run
He turned around, so that left none.

**Sarah Alford  (8)**
**Marchwood Junior School**

# Little Kittens

Five little kittens ran through the door
One got stuck, so that left four.

Four little kittens ran in and hit my knee
One hit its head, so that left three.

Three little kittens ate my shoe
One choked, so that left two.

Two little kittens playing with a gun
One shot himself, so that left one.

One little kitten playing with his mum
She fell off, so that left none.

**Emma Stokes  (9)**
**Marchwood Junior School**


# Five Little Kittens

Five little kittens went out of the door
One got lost, so that left four.

Four little kittens went out to sea
One swam too far away, so that left three.

Three little kittens went to the zoo,
One joined the circus, so that left two.

Two little kittens went for a run,
One ran away, so that left one.

One little kitten did not have much fun,
Broke her leg and that left none.

**Hannah Reader  (8)**
**Marchwood Junior School**

# What Is Brown?

What is brown? A tree trunk is brown,
The leaves shining like a golden crown.

What is black? A hair is black,
The hairdressers go back.

What is white? A cloud is white,
Drifting through the night.

What is grey? A jumper is grey,
From Marchwood Junior School in the day.

**Vilisi Tekei (9)**
Marchwood Junior School


# What Is Brown?

What is brown? A tree trunk is brown.
As big as a greyhound.
What is grey? A tie is grey
Like a rainy day.
What is black? A hole is black
A bit like tarmac.
What is gold? The sun is gold
Shining over all I've told.

**Emma Poulton (8)**
Marchwood Junior School


# Red

Red looks like a glittering Somerset sunset
Red tastes like fizzing cherryade
Red feels like burning hot fire from a dragon
Red sounds like a red Indian song
Red smells like hot delicious chocolate.

**Laura Bradford (8)**
Marchwood Junior School

# Special Penguins

Five special penguins went to explore
One fell off a cliff, so that left four.

Four special penguins found a key
One locked himself in, so that left three.

Three special penguins went to the zoo
One got eaten so that left two.

Two special penguins went to see their mum
One got slobbered on, so that left one.

One special penguin went to run
Tripped in a skip, so that left none.

**Emily Macdonald (8)**
**Marchwood Junior School**


# Purple

Purple smells like a crushed rose on a summer's day.
Purple tastes like a fizzy blackcurrant sweet.
Purple feels like riding on a horseback on a winter's day.
Purple looks like ponies mucking about in the yard.
Purple sounds like thunder behind a sunset.

**Leila Clelland (9)**
**Marchwood Junior School**


# Yellow

Yellow smells like a sunny summer's day
Yellow tastes like the flavour of a lemon
Yellow feels like something long and bumpy
Yellow looks like the biggest and most faraway star
Yellow sounds like a funny sort of person.

**Jimmy McHugh (9)**
**Marchwood Junior School**

# What Is Gold?

What is gold? An eagle is gold.
Flying from its hold.

What is brown? A chocolate is brown
And it is a noun.

What is white? A snowdrop is white
Falling in the dark night.

What is grey? A rainy day is grey
Just like a drey.

What is black? Coal is black
That is old like my dad's muddy sack.

**Emily Hinton  (8)**
**Marchwood Junior School**


# What Is Gold

What is gold? The sun is gold
It is so old.

What is grey? The clouds are grey
All on a drizzly day.

What is white? The white board is white
Shining really bright.

What is brown? A dog is brown
With a great big frown.

What is black? Your name is black
Written on a sack.

**Jenny White  (9)**
**Marchwood Junior School**

# Special Penguins

Five special penguins went to explore
One fell off a cliff, so that left four.

Four special penguins found a key
One locked himself in, so that left three.

Three special penguins went to the zoo
One got eaten, so that left two.

Two special penguins went to see their mum,
One got slobbered on, so that left one.

One special penguin went for a run
Tripped in a skip, so that left none.

**Sophie Manser  (8)**
**Marchwood Junior School**


# Steaming Devils

Five steaming devils broke the law
One went to prison, so that left four.

Four steaming devils broke their knee
One went to hospital so that left three.

Three steaming devils got stuck in a queue
One got bored so that left two.

Two steaming devils had a bun
One had poison in, so that left one.

One steaming devil had a journey to the sun
He ran out of fuel, so that left none.

**Holly Swanton  (9)**
**Marchwood Junior School**

# Ducks

Five stupid ducks went walking to the door
One went out so that left four.
Four stupid ducks went to have a cup of tea
One ran off so that left three.
Three stupid ducks went to the zoo
One stayed there so that left two.
Two stupid ducks went to the sea
One had a bun, so that left one.
One stupid duck went to have fun
He got lost, so that left none.

**Elizabeth Seary  (9)**
Marchwood Junior School


# Parcels

Five pink parcels went to score
One came unwrapped, so that left four.
Four pink parcels set sail to sea
One fell in, so that left three.
Three pink parcels went to the loo
One got flushed, so that left two.
Two pink parcels went to the fair for some fun
One stopped to buy balloons, so that left one.
One pink parcel went out for a bun
Lost his way home, so that left none.

**Emily Campion  (8)**
Marchwood Junior School


# Blue

Blue smells like salted water on the beach.
Blue tastes like a juicy blueberry melting in my mouth.
Blue feels like wind quietly going past my face.
Blue looks like a very calm sea.
Blue sounds like waves crashing against the rocks.

**Beth Harney  (9)**
Marchwood Junior School

# Little Kittens

Five little kittens ran through the door
One got stuck, so that left four.
Four little kittens ran in and hit my knee
One hit his head, so that left three.
Three little kittens ate my shoe
One choked, and that left two.
Two little kittens playing with a gun
One shot himself so that left one.
One little kitten playing with its mum
She fell, so that left none.

**Sally Pitcher (8)**
**Marchwood Junior School**


# Elephant

An elephant has . . .
Eyes like a tiny black button
Legs like an oak tree trunk
Ears like a bouncy beach ball.
A trunk like a dangerous snake.

An elephant is . . .
As wrinkled as a slept in bed
As slow as a loaded camel
As heavy as a giant
As strong as an iron pole.

**Calem Amminin (8)**
**Marchwood Junior School**


# Gold

Gold smells like golden syrup pouring on pancakes.
Gold tastes like butter on the end of my tongue.
Gold feels like a wedding dress falling on the floor.
Gold looks like the golden work sign on the board.
Gold sounds like a sparkler in a kid's hand.

**Sian Sayce (9)**
**Marchwood Junior School**

# Elephant

An elephant has . . .
Eyes like a brown small bead
Legs like a metre stick
Ears like four pieces of very flappy paper
A trunk that is massive
A memory like an enormous thesaurus.

An elephant is . . .
As wrinkled as a pleated curtain
As stately as a royal queen
As slow as a slippery slug
As heavy as a tunnel of metal
As strong as a fighting Indian.

**Joseph Whitfield  (8)**
**Marchwood Junior School**


# An Elephant

An elephant has . . .
Eyes like a small pothole
Legs like a fat encyclopaedia
Ears like a thin pancake
A trunk like a thick clock
A memory like a long measuring tape.

An elephant is . . .
As wrinkled as a bed cover
As stately as a birthday party
As slow as a tortoise
As heavy as 1000 bricks
As strong as a piece of steel.

**Tyler Burgin  (8)**
**Marchwood Junior School**

# Elephant

An elephant has . . .
Eyes like weeny washers
Legs like the Empire State Building
Ears like ginormous white boards
A trunk like a twisted old willow tree
A memory like Einstein.

An elephant is . . .
As wrinkled as twenty old men put together
As stately as proud Prince Harry
As slow as a snail on a freezing frosty day
As heavy as a thousand pound weight
As strong as an ancient old oak tree
As tall as sixty schools put together
As dirty as thick thirty inch mud
As dry as a rusty old go kart.

**Joe White  (9)**
**Marchwood Junior School**


# Elephant

An elephant has . . .
Eyes like a tiny light bulb
Legs like an old oak tree, sixteen years old
Ears like an eagle's biggest wing
A trunk like a small staircase in a hospital.
A memory like a goldfish.

An elephant is . . .
As wrinkled as a dry prawn
As stately as a royal queen so proud
As slow as a tortoise so slow
As heavy as sixteen houses
As strong as forty hospitals.

**Laura Rangecroft  (8)**
**Marchwood Junior School**

# Elephant

An elephant has . . .
Eyes like tiny cherries
Legs like a trunk from an old oak tree
Ears like giant pancakes
A trunk like a thick piece of rope
A memory like a wise scientist

An elephant is . . .
As wrinkled as an old tired man
As stately as a posh queen
As slow as the slowest tortoise in the world
As heavy as a world's strongest wrestler
As strong as the strongest man.

**Chelsea Ayres  (9)**
**Marchwood Junior School**


# An Elephant

An elephant has . . .
Eyes like small pancakes
Legs like enormous tree trunks
Ears like bent pancakes
A trunk like a curly crinkly chip
A memory like a giant apple.

An elephant is . . .
As wrinkled as an old woman
As stately as a roly king
As slow as a peacock
As heavy as two trees
As strong as a big monster.

**Stacey Pettman  (9)**
**Marchwood Junior School**

# Stripy Zebras

Five stripy zebras galloping through the door
One got smacked, so that left four.

Four stripy zebras got stung by a bee
One got stung badly, so that left three.

Three stripy zebras playing hide and seek
One shouted *boo!* So that left two.

Two stripy zebras eating a bun
One got messy, so that left one.

One stripy zebra lost its mum
He went to find her, so that left none.

**Chloe Meredith & Amy Pickford  (9)**
**Marchwood Junior School**


# Fat Gorillas

Five fat gorillas went off to explore
One fell off a cliff, so that left four.

Four fat gorillas sat on a tree
One fell off, and broke his knee, that left three.

Three fat gorillas put on a shoe
One toppled over, so that left two.

Two fat gorillas ate a plum,
One began to choke, so that left one.

One fat gorilla went to have some fun,
He slipped and broke his leg, so that left none.

**Shanice Lund  (9)**
**Marchwood Junior School**

# Small Aliens

Five little aliens broke the law
One was speeding, so that left four.

Four small aliens all hurt their knee
One knee was broken, so that left three.

Three small aliens found a didgeridoo
One got stuck, so that left two.

Two small aliens had a gun
One shot his friend, so that left one.

One small alien found his mum
He ran away, so that left none.

**Elliot Ireland  (9)**
Marchwood Junior School


# Pink

Pink smells like a rose in the swaying breeze.
Pink tastes like steamed lobster.
Pink feels like bursting fireworks in my hand.
Pink looks like a ball dress at a ball.
Pink sounds like tassels jangling in a dance.

**Sarah White  (8)**
Marchwood Junior School


# Blue

Blue smells like a lake gleaming in the sunlight.
Blue sounds like boiling water.
Blue looks like the sky floating around.
Blue feels like soft leather.
Blue tastes like crunchy leaves.

**Jamie Passfield  (8)**
Marchwood Junior School

# The Playground

The playground can be rough,
The playground can be tough,
The footballs fly,
Then children cry,
It's all about growing up.

Lunch is over,
We all run outside,
The boys scare them,
Then the girls hide,
The boys want to find them; they all divide.

They check behind the dustbins,
Behind the old oak tree,
The girls are good at hiding,
Where on Earth could they be?
There's only one more place to check,
Up the old oak tree.

The boys eventually find them,
Sitting in the tree,
Their hiding game they gave away,
By giggling,
*Te he! Te he! Te he!*

**Harvey Meeds  (10)**
**Marycourt School**


# Jelly Beans

Jelly beans, jelly beans in a glass jar,
Looking like a coloured window from afar,
All yummy and tasty,
One by one they slowly go,
Then they are *gone!*

**Alex Sharp  (9)**
**Marycourt School**

# The Zoo

We're going to the zoo, zoo, zoo,
Whatever can we do, do, do?
Party with the pythons,
Bounce with the bears,
Tickle the tigers,
That's what we can do!

We're going to the zoo, zoo, zoo,
Whatever can we eat, eat, eat?
Salty sausages,
Bumper burgers,
And chunky chips,
That's what we can eat!

We're going to the zoo, zoo, zoo,
Whatever can we drink, drink, drink?
Fizzy Fanta,
Magnificent milkshake,
Lovely lemonade,
That's what we can drink!

**Annabelle Mackay (9)**
**Marycourt School**


# The Fire Phoenix

Fire is a glowing phoenix,
Whose feathers shine like lightning,
The phoenix burns and burns until put out
By lashing water,
When the phoenix comes it brings worries with it,
Dragging the worries over everyone,
Crackling away like a party cracker,
Flashing and flashing until the lashing water comes.

**Charis White (10)**
**Marycourt School**

# Happiness Is Kind

Happiness is bright yellow like bursting into song,
Happiness sounds like a song in the spring,
Happiness looks like the colours of the rainbow,
Happiness tastes like a sweet taste,
Happiness feels like a soft teddy,
Happiness reminds me of being tucked up in bed and
Mum and Dad say goodnight.

**Madison Roberts (8)**
**Marycourt School**

# Going Nowhere

A tank trundles up the hill,
A red racing car zooms through town,
A huge double-decker bus passes smoothly by,
An extremely fast motorbike speeds past,
A lorry with a heavy load heads down town,
They're all going the other way and I am stuck
In a traffic jam.

**Jack Willetts (8)**
**Marycourt School**

# A Dream

I turned off my slippers and put on my light.
I went down my breakfast and ate my stairs.
I clean my clothes and put on my teeth.
I put on my door and opened the jacket.
I got into the school and went to car.

*And some dreams*
*Are very*
*Confusing.*

**Jake Dicken (9)**
**Marycourt School**

# Catherine Wheel

Colourful Catherines curl,
Around,
They go,
Helter-skelters aren't as good,
Enjoyable,
Really exciting to do,
Interesting fun to have,
Never forget today,
Enchanting, enjoyable world.

When were these made up,
Heaven has given us enjoyment,
Eye-catching colours,
Enter my favourite day,
Let it never end.

**Robin White  (8)**
**Marycourt School**


# Mad Excuses

A bomb landed in my bedroom,
My toilet wouldn't open,
I ran out of spoons and bowls,
My uniform was stolen by burglars,
The police had my toothpaste in jail!
My cup caught fire,
The door was covered in bugs,
Dad's car blew up,
There was a huge traffic jam.
My friends say it's cool . . .
And that's why I'm late for school!

**Andrew Vincent  (9)**
**Marycourt School**

# Fire Tiger

A tiger burns with fire,
As it climbs up high the fire follows,
It never shows any mercy,
It's big and wide like a firewall.

The tiger burns with fear and fury,
Never has it liked wood,
Its arch enemy is only water,
But when they are swept away,
They shall burn another day.

**Thomas Battersby  (9)**
**Marycourt School**


# The Lion Fire

The fire is a ferocious lion,
It's hot and red,
It strikes with no warning
With his roar,
The popping wood falls to the ground
And burn, burn, burn.
The roar of the dead
It licks the hot air.

**Ben Lewis  (10)**
**Marycourt School**


# The Scorpion

As the scorpion walks it makes
A crackling sound like a fire.
He stings like a fire
Burning his pinches are like when
A fire takes down a house.

**Joe Podmore  (10)**
**Marycourt School**

# Fire!

Fire is a salamander flicking up and down,
It runs round the logs and flares up quite high.
Round and round it spins.
End of the fire, the salamander dies and the light goes out.

**Yiannis Panou  (9)**
**Marycourt School**


# Drowning In Guilt

Wanting to burrow under my pillow,
My face turning red,
I feel so bad for what I've done,
It fills me up with dread.

It was great the feeling I had,
Just a minute ago,
I was leaping with joy,
When trouble started to grow.

Staring at the pillow on the floor,
I can't believe I did it,
What were the thoughts that came to my head?
It fills me up with guilt.

I am scared like a fox being hunted,
My eyes swelling up red,
Blinking away my tears,
I can't believe that she's dead.

**Bethany Goodchild  (11)**
**Newbridge Junior School**

# Hatred

All the nasty names they call me
Are going through my head
Steam blowing out my ears
My face is turning red

It's getting into my mind
Tapping at my brain
I was so happy yesterday
But I just don't feel the same

They're standing all around me
But shouting at me too
I can't believe it happened
I don't know what to do

Stop laughing at me
I want to be alone
Can't you see?
I want to go home

I start to run away
Tears run down my face
I'm not sure where I'm going
But it's got to be better than this place

And now I'm back at home
Away from all the sorrow
But it won't last long
It'll start again tomorrow.

**Rhiannon Smithard  (11)**
**Newbridge Junior School**

# Computers Are My Favourite Things

Computers are fun
They are easy as pie
I like computers
They will never lie

Computers are electrical
Computers are spantifical
Computers are great
They are new technology

Games are really fun
I play them with my chums
Games are cool
I want to have them all

We all like a game
They all have different aims
Games are really fun
I play them with my chums.

**Thomas Arnfeld (10)**
**Newbridge Junior School**


# Happy Is Not Me!

Looking across the playground,
What do I see?
I see people staring at me.

Just wanting to be free,
Happy is a thing I want to be.

All of the people in little groups,
I want to join them,
But my mood just droops.

I just mope about,
I always want to shout,
*Make me happy!*

**Katie Heap  (11)**
**Newbridge Junior School**

# Feelings

Anger is dark colours merged together,
Anger is silent but strong,
Anger repeats in your head,
Anger builds up like a volcano,
Anger lives in you.

Jealousy is competitive,
Jealousy is being left out,
Jealousy is being spiteful,
Jealousy is envy,
Jealousy is sibling rivalry.

Fear is being scared,
Fear is being caught,
Fear is the unknown,
Fear is being nervous,
Fear is phobia.

Sadness is depression,
Sadness is loneliness,
Sadness is being devastated,
Sadness is disbelief,
Sadness is hurtful,

Guilt is horrid,
Guilt is feeling down,
Guilt is being worried,
Guilt is regretting,
Guilt is in your heart.

Happiness is being kind,
Happiness is being thoughtful,
Happiness is being grateful,
Happiness is eating chocolate,
Happiness is being praised.

**Melissa Peck  (11)**
**Newbridge Junior School**

# My Favourite Things

My favourite things to do are . . .

Jumping in a swimming pool,
Swimming round and up and down,
Diving down to touch the ground.

My favourite things to do are . . .

Playing in the garden,
Jumping round like I'm really mad,
Playing on my happy, loving dad.

My favourite things to do are . . .

Watching my favourite TV show,
Staring at baby lion cubs,
While eating ice cream out of the tub.

My favourite things to do are . . .

Going out and having fun,
Walking on a warm summer's beach,
Eating a yummy, scrummy, lovely peach,

But most of all I do love
My family most of all.

**Yasmin Wells  (11)**
**Newbridge Junior School**

# My Favourite Things

My favourite things are . . .
Chocolate in gallons,
Reading my books,
Slobbing in bed,
And having good looks,

Pizza to eat,
Slice after slice,
Ice cream is next,
With a touch of strong spice,

'Hanging' with friends,
Having good fun,
Then it's straight to the beach,
To laze in the sun,

Popcorn and drinks,
The cinema's great,
Then it's time for tea,
Food piled on my plate,

But these are my favourite things,
What are yours?

**Madeline Goodchild  (11)**
**Newbridge Junior School**

# I'm Bored, Bored and Bored

I'm bored, bored and bored
Like a house with no roof
Like a phone without a SIM card
Like a pencil without lead
A pen without any ink

I'm bored, bored and bored
Like a book with no pages
A face without eyes
Like an ocean without water
Like a pen without a lid

I'm bored, bored and bored
Like a pitiful sink without taps
A forsaken boat without sails
Like fingers without nails
Like a mouth without teeth

I'm bored, bored and bored
Like a vein without blood
A head without a nose
Like a book without a front cover
Like a house without windows

I'm bored, bored and bored
Like a room without walls
Like a field without grass
Like a body with no heart
I'm bored, bored and bored.

**Amber Privett (10)**
**Newbridge Junior School**

# From Good To Bad

I love a lot of things
Clothes and shoes
And gold diamond rings
What else, who knows

Toys and make up
A total new makeover
Reading, writing
And riding my dad's Land Rover

My favourite is my friends
And when I'm fed
I also love
A soft pillow against my head

I love swimming
Right to the bottom
With my piggy little brother
Who can be so rotten

That was a long time ago

I hadn't meant to do it
It was only a bit of fun
I am dumb, I am stupid
And now my time has come

I close my eyes
There he lies
Weak and limp
Then I die.

**Samantha Chearman  (11)**
**Newbridge Junior School**

# Anger

Niggled by name calling
Face getting red
Building up stress
Body starting to shake

Smoke coming from my ears
Eyes getting narrow
Veins getting blue
And brain starting to erupt

I'm losing my temper now
Stop bullying me
Or I'll call my big brother
Let me go you bully

Fist getting ready to punch
And punching him round the face
Foot getting ready to kick
And kicking him round the stomach

I'm sorry, I'm sorry I punched you
I didn't mean to do it
But you pushed me to do it.

**Vuyani Ncube  (10)**
**Newbridge Junior School**

# Affecting The Future

There was a man named Dean
Who was extremely keen
On making a time machine

So he screwed and he wired
And later he hired
A friend to test his machine

Unfortunately he fell in
As the machine made a terrible din
And whizzed him to the 25th century

But he wasn't liking what he had seen
So switch to friendly and green
For poor old Dean
Who saw the Earth polluted

Where cars dominated the roads
And polluted the sky
With loads of unnatural gasses

And people coughing and spluttering
Over a very dangerous something
Hanging in the sky.

**Jordan Jones  (11)**
**Newbridge Junior School**

# Bored

My mate has got a new friend
I have no friends about
They're all stuck in referral
I feel really left out

I'm now losing my mind
Over a silly boy called Bob
His head is so average
But as round as a door knob

It's time to get angry
Bob must be destroyed
But if I do
My mate will be annoyed

I've found a way
To get my payback
I need a new friend
How about Jack.

**Jamie Hale (10)**
**Newbridge Junior School**


# Black

Black is the night, dark and mysterious
An evil dragon burning a house
Black is the colour
Of a gun denting a wall
A black wizard zapping a mouse
Black is a poison so very deadly
Black is ink splodging all over my work
But you couldn't live without it.

**Jacob Morrison (9)**
**Portway Junior School**

# Arsenal Vs Man Utd

Here we are at Highbury,
Cheering on our team,
Man U don't stand a chance,
Against the Gunners, thick and mean!

The whistle goes for kick-off,
Vieira with the ball,
Passes it to Fabregas,
Man U looking small.

Here comes Rooney up the wing,
Passes it to Scholes,
Scholes hits it hard into the goal,
Arsenal need some goals!

The whistle goes for half-time,
Here we go again,
Pires shoots it over the goalie's head,
Man U are starting to bend!

5 minutes till the end,
Fabregas gets the pass,
Heads it over goalie,
Arsenal have some class!

**Jack Copping  (8)**
**Portway Junior School**

# Blue

Blue is a mint that's really nice
Blue is a background that I have in my bedroom
Blue is a swimming pool that I play in
Blue is a uniform that I wear for school
Blue is when you get punched in the eye
Blue is ink that comes out of a pen
Blue is the sky that is light blue.

**Ben Cox  (8)**
**Portway Junior School**

# Blue

Blue is the stormy sea,
Blue is the cloudy sky,

Blue is the swimming pool,
Blue is the freezing cold,

Blue is the splatted ink on your page,

Blue is the colour of our display board,
Blue is the colour of our walls,

Blue is the colour of Mrs Marriott's cupboard,
Blue is the colour of Southampton's away kit,
Blue is the colour of my journal,
Blue is my favourite colour of all.

**Ella Howells  (8)**
**Portway Junior School**


# Black

Black is the fur of a spider
Black is the dark night
Black is a shadow
Black is a sky full of darkness
Black is evil and having a war or fight
Black is anger inside your body
Black is the colour of a dark cape.

**Henry Edwards  (8)**
**Portway Junior School**


# Yellow

Yellow is a burning sun from the high up sky
Yellow is the car whooshing as fast as a dart
Yellow is the colour of a mug and it is also the colour to have fun
Yellow is the one to show the way
Yellow is the colour of wool from a jumper as well.

**James Duff (9)**
**Portway Junior School**

# Double Double

*(Inspired by 'Macbeth')*

Double, double, toil and trouble
Fire burn and cauldron bubble
Feather of an eagle, claw of a dragon
Come on cauldron double bubble
Hunter's dagger dripping with blood
A guilty conscience like a devil

Double, double, toil and trouble
Fire burn and cauldron bubble
Lion's fur and a leech alive
Sizzle, sizzle cauldron
Smell of rose, poison rose
And ice as hot as fire

Double, double, toil and trouble
Fire burn and cauldron bubble
Eye of a wolf and heart of snake
Come on cauldron bubble and bake
Macbeth, Macduff murders Macbeth
Kill them, kill them, kill them.

**Sophie Roberts**
**Portway Junior School**


# My Poem

Here I sit on the rubble-strewn ground
I hate the black sky
I gaze around at the scene of destruction
I hate that my family and friends have all gone
I need to have shelter and someone to look after me

Here I sit on the rubble-strewn ground
Loneliness haunts me like a fading ghost
I gaze around at the scene of destruction
Desolation stretches ahead, along a never-ending road
Who will care for me now?

**Charlie Blackmore  (10)**
**Portway Junior School**

# What Is Fear?

Fear is something
That creeps up behind you
Fear has a voice
That goes *whooooo!*

Fear is something
That's in your head
When you're tucked
Sleepily in bed

Darkness has a name
Fear has a name
For you never know
If it really came

Gardens are nice
Maths has a dice
But fear is horrid
All inside your head.

**Gillian Parker  (9)**
**Portway Junior School**

# Blue

Blue is cold,
That makes me shiver.
Blue is a bluebell,
Swishing in the wind.
Blue is a bright blue sky,
I see in summer.
Blue is my school uniform,
I wear each day.
Blue is ink,
Splodgy and wet.
Blue is the colour of my car,
Shining in the sun.
Blue is the sea,
Sploshing about.

**Luke Robbins  (9)**
**Portway Junior School**

# Blue

Blue is the colour
Of a bright blue sky
Blue is cold
And makes me shiver
Blue is the sea
Sparkling in the sun
Blue is the colour
When you bruise your knee
Blue is a new car
Shiny and cool
Blue is the ink
That splodges on my work
Blue is a bluebell
In the spring
Blue is the colour
Of my school uniform
But I can't imagine
Living without it.

**James Holder  (9)**
**Portway Junior School**


# Black

Black is the
Road where cars
Roll along.
My pencil case is black
And bumpy all over.
Black is the ink that
Splodges over my page.
Black is the colour of the CD player,
Black is the colour of the night,
And black are the tyres on cars.

**Christopher Speed  (8)**
**Portway Junior School**

# Blue

Blue is a colour bright and bold,
Blue is a colour on the horizon's hold.
Blue is a swimming pool, nice and cool,
Blue is my uniform I wear to school.
Blue is a blue tit singing a song,
Blue is a colour when you feel cold.
Blue is a blueberry that squishes in my mouth,
Blue is a colour on the wall of my house.
Blue is a colour in my class,
Blue is a colour that makes me go fast.

**Anna-Leigh Brookes (8)**
**Portway Junior School**


# Blue

Blue is the colour of the sea,
Blue is the colour of Portway's school uniform,
Blue is the colour you turn when you are cold,
Blue is a colour that you write with,
Blue is the colour of a car,
Blue is the colour of a mint,
Blue is the colour of a sharp pen,
Blue is the colour of a whale.

**Lewis Parkinson (9)**
**Portway Junior School**


# Blue

Blue is the world that we behold
Blue is a book into which we look
Blue is a shirt that will not hurt
Blue is an ink that could sink
Blue is the sea that we see
Blue is the day that says, 'Hip hip hooray.'

**Lewis Nicholls (8)**
**Portway Junior School**

# Blue

Blue is a wrapping paper that wraps presents in
Blue is a signal that says 'be careful'
Blue is a paint that scatters around
Blue is a big trampoline I bounce on
Blue is a swimming pool that I feel under my feet
Blue is a blue, blue sea that says hello to me
Blue is a cold shower running up my spine
Blue is when I feel sick
Blue is my toothpaste that I use
Blue is my uniform I wear to school
Blue is the ink that splats everywhere
The blueberries I eat are so juicy, yummy
Blue is the colour that you feel when you're sad
Blue is the colour of a seal
Blue is the bright sky with birds flying high
Blue is a bright star above
Blue is always there with you
Blue is the best colour of all.

**Kerry Rookes  (9)**
**Portway Junior School**


# Everything Is Blue

Blue is the colour of the high clear sky
Blue is the colour of blueberry pie
Blue is the colour that splats from the sink
Blue is the colour that I drink
The colour that I am when I'm cold
The colour with a heart of gold
Blue is the colour that smudges on my page
Blue is the colour trapped in my cage
The colour of a great big whale
That splashes its beautiful tail
Blue is a colour I wear in every way
Blue is a colour that saves the day!

**Carmen Broome  (8)**
**Portway Junior School**

# World War II

All that could be heard was the deafening bombing
The outrageous screaming
The upsetting screaming
Children crying over their parents
Soldiers falling to the floor
The miserable results of a terrible war

In the sky, were the planes
This war was not just fun and games
As British soldiers prepared to fight
Families ran with all their might
Lights spiralling round and round
As bombers twisted to the ground

As explosions landed in the street
Air raid shelters gathered heat
People worried, whimpering with fear
Would their lives end now and here?
Terror suffocated all of the town
And people just wondered what would happen to them now?

**Ashleigh Gurd (11)**
**Portway Junior School**


# My Tsunami Poem

It sounds like the shatter of so many people's hearts
As they lose their loved ones

A wreck, dead bodies everywhere, so unhappy, droopy and sad
That's what it looks like

It feels like a wet and cold unlively place
People scrambling to safety, people falling as they run

It tastes like a cold, salty stream of tears
Running away from the waves that killed so many

An earthquake is like a mist of people running to keep their lives
But so many were killed and lost.

**Emma Hine (10)**
**Portway Junior School**

# White

White is the colour of a frosty morning
White is the colour of a snowy winter's day
White is the colour of my brand new page
Ready for my story to begin
White is the colour of the clouds passing by
White is the colour of pure white snowdrops and the sign of spring
White is the colour of a foggy morning
White is the colour that I turn as I feel a shiver down my spine
White is the calmest colour of all, my favourite!

**Zoe Russell (8)**
**Portway Junior School**


# My Terrible Life Of Mine

Here I sit with no family and no food to help me to survive
Memories stand next to me with the big sun melting through my weak
body
I look around while I think; where is my family?
Will I survive this rubble on the sand?

These memories breaking my heart whilst the water crashes
Right through my ragged body

Who will care for me now?

**Amy Cutting  (10)**
**Portway Junior School**


# Help!

I sit here in the cramped hospital
Hungry as an eagle to get better and forget, forget
Screaming, shouting from the pain and stress
My memories are big but I was hungry to forget, to forget
Where are my rights?
I respect, have responsibilities, but no rights!

**Anna Bazzoni  (8)**
**Portway Junior School**

# What Is Yellow?

Yellow is a colour that is very warm
Yellow is a colour that feels like a swarm
Yellow is part of a very important fire
That makes you feel like a wire
Yellow is a colour blazing from the sun
That isn't meaning to think like a strong, fierce hun
Yellow is a very posh little pose
It is also part of a tiny suit of clothes
Yellow is a food called cheese
That gives a tender, tasty ease
Yellow is a part of a pretty daisy
That gives you the names of Ellie and Maisy
Yellow is a colour very strong and fit
But can you imagine living without it?

**Amy Potts  (8)**
**Portway Junior School**


# Blue

Blue is an ink pen that you write with at school
Blue is the blue tit singing at the morning
Blue is the blue whale singing to the sun
Blue is my jumper that I wear to my school
Blue is a cold feeling that you get inside
Blue is a dolphin leaping so high
Blue is a hairband, squishy and soft
Blue is the peacock showing his feathers
Blue is the blue, blue sky and
Blue is the colour of someone else's blue eyes
Blue is the colour of the shimmering waterfall
Blue is one colour in the rainbow so high!

**Jeanette Treacy  (8)**
**Portway Junior School**

# Soldiers

The rapid fire of bullets filled my ears
People dying, people screaming, they're all in fear
The bombs dropping down, they're so loud
The dog fights in the sky, there's a lot of sound

People can see the opposite side's head getting blown off
They're running and crying, wishing they were in their loft
Spitfires are circling the opposite team
The bombs that they are shooting are so shiny and clean

They can feel the blood squirting out from a friend
The guts, the brains, it's like it will never ever end
The cold and strong wind splats on my head
All the people suffering, most of them are dead.

**Owen Young  (11)**
**Portway Junior School**


# What I Felt Like After The Tsunami!

Here I walk on the rubble blocked road
Weakness comes to me, like my frozen blood
I look around for someone to speak to
Weakness is terror running to my brain
Will anyone find me? Is anyone here?

I am worried about my life
My hunger makes my tummy growl like a nasty bear in a forest
I'm looking for the ruins of my house to make me remember
My hunger is my mother's beauty I will never see again
Someone find me? Someone help me?

**Victoria Collyer  (10)**
**Portway Junior School**

# My Terrible Life

Here I lay, injured on the dirty rubble
Loneliness is like a black cloud, never to fade away
I can't see any buildings or people
The loneliness in my heart is a black stone, aching and aching
Who will love and care for me now?
I run away from the ghost in my mind
I'm fearless like a wolf in the moonlit sky
I can hear and see people crying
I'm fearless, I'm a brave lion
Who will stand up for me now?

**Bena Tymms (10)**
**Portway Junior School**


# Rainbow

Red is blood running through your veins
Yellow is the sun, hot on your skin
Pink is a flower sat in the ground
Green is the grass, long and wild
Orange is a crab sat on the beach
Purple is a bruise when you have been hit
Blue is the sky where the clouds sit
I am a rainbow and that is it.

**Sarah Shehata (9)**
**Portway Junior School**


# Blue

Blue is the colour of a fish that I named Cit
Blue is the ocean with a ship sailing on it
Blue is a ball bouncing in the air
Blue is a ghost that isn't really there
Blue is the air that we breathe
Blue is a restaurant that you leave.

**Caelan Burnett (8)**
**Portway Junior School**

# My Poem

Here I sit on the rubble-strewn ground
Loneliness haunts me like a dark never-ending hole
I gaze around at the rubble
Desolation stretches ahead, a long never-ending road
Who will care for me now?
Here I lay with bad memories corked into my head
My memories are of my family and the tsunami
I stare at the scene of destruction
My loss of my friends and family
Who will care for me now?

**Jordan O'Connor  (10)**
**Portway Junior School**


# What Is Kind?

Kindness is sharing all of my jokes
Kindness is laughter, big, funny and loved
Kindness is a rainbow, all different colours
Kindness is fun
Kindness is playing with others when they're alone
Kindness is being helpful
Kindness is when you're friendly
Like helping people when they're hurt
You have to be kind.

**Christopher Tanner  (8)**
**Portway Junior School**


# Love Is

Love is gentle, kind and soft
Love is a rainbow that looks down at you
Love is a smell of a sweet, sweet flower
Love is mistletoe, your first kiss at Christmas
Love is always around you in the air
Love is the one you want, no doubt about it.

**Amanda Brown  (9)**
**Portway Junior School**

# World War II

World War II has started
World War II is here
World War II will never end
Or so it seems to me

Bombs are soaring down to Earth
Bombs are smashing into houses
Bombs are flinging out from planes
Oh please don't land on me

Screaming from the sirens
Screaming from the people
Screaming from the bombs
Oh what a lot of noise

Andersons made from tin
Andersons all full
Andersons all stiff and hard
But that Anderson couldn't save them.

**Cristina Trowbridge  (10)**
**Portway Junior School**


# Asia Destroyed

Here I sit on the rubble-strewn ground
Memories are like a big black hole sucking up
I look around at the destroyed land
Memories are a black hole
My rights have been washed away

Here I am starving on the destroyed beach
My weakness is like a monster
I look around and I'm still worried
Weakness is a pain in my heart
My respect has been stolen from me.

**Mitchell Webber  (9)**
**Portway Junior School**

# World War II

In the easy, fiery red
People's hearts being filled with dread
Up in the sky, soldiers still fight
As they use up all their might
People are killing, people are dying
Children being hurt, you can hear them crying

As the bombs drop onto the street
Listen carefully, you can hear the tap of their feet
In the night you just can't sleep
So get out of bed and look at the streets
You can still hear the sirens but you can't hear the screams
I think everyone is still in their dreams

The German planes have now gone
But I still think of the bombs
Before the street looked its best
But at last I can rest.

**Kayleigh Lewis  (10)**
**Portway Junior School**


# My Worst Nightmare!

Here I sleep on the rubble-strewn ground
Memories are like fading grey horses in the distance
I stand watching my family being washed away
My hunger was a rumble of thunder
I have a right to be looked after and cared for!

I'm worried, there looking at the ground, worrying about my family
Loneliness is like a ghost fading away
I hate to think how my mum and dad felt
Hate was unbearable as my heart turned into stone
I do have the right to be protected and have an education!

But how long will this take?

**Kim Willis  (9)**
**Portway Junior School**

# Clock

I'm a clock on the wall
I tick, I tock
I point to one
I point to three
When I point to twelve
It means it's lunchtime
It's eight o'clock, now it's bedtime
Bye-bye, tick . . . tock . . . tick . . . tock.

**Floyd Steele  (8)**
**Portway Junior School**


# What Is Pink And Violet?

Pink is love all around
It's a feeling in your head
Violet is the colour of my face
When I'm embarrassed
Pink is like a delicious pudding
You might eat me for your dessert
I'm your lips, I'm your heart
I'm a big jam tart.

**Chelsey Goddard  (9)**
**Portway Junior School**


# Earthquake

It looks like a bowl of Frosties.
It tastes like an old egg.
An earthquake is black
It smells like a very, very old sock.
It feels like a stab in the back.
It sounds like a heart beating.

**Luis Zeffertt  (10)**
**Portway Junior School**

# Witches' Spell

*(Inspired by 'Macbeth')*

*Double, double, toil and trouble*
*Fire burn and cauldron bubble*
The spit of an adder
A fat cat's tail
The teacher's cold bladder
And a bottle of ale
The dog's liver melts
And the double fire beams
When the smell of the swamp
And the witches evilly scream
The wolf's slimy tooth begins to crack
And the vocal chords huddle
When the cat's spine snaps
*Double, double, toil and trouble*
*Fire burn and cauldron bubble*
You shall be in a lot of trouble!

**Joseph Lindridge  (9)**
**Portway Junior School**


# Happiness Is . . .

Happiness is laughter
When Christopher falls off his chair
A joke, which is funny
Sometimes to share

Happiness is friendliness
When you are friends
You sometimes play games
Which is fair
And when Chris has wacky hair

Happiness is love
When you are loved.

**Bradley Buckwell  (9)**
**Portway Junior School**

# Earthquake

It looks like a lovely village at first
And then an earthquake struck
And now it looks like a sea of bodies
And people have lost their lives
And loved ones

It sounds like a whole world of dynamite
Going off at the same time and
People screaming for their lives

It tastes like a lovely curry before
And now it tastes like muddy water with some salty tears

It feels like rubbish and rubble
Hitting your body at high speed

It smells like some lovely curries and then it's putrid

Earthquake is like a brown sea after the mud has fallen in the water
Like someone tripping over.

**Luke Ginger  (10)**
**Portway Junior School**


# The Colours And What They Are

Black is the darkness colour
Blue is the coldness colour
Red is the colour of anger that races through your head
Yellow is a heat that feels like the sun

Amber is lightning that's in the dark night
White is snow that makes you freeze up

Orange looks like lava gushing from a volcano
Grey is a tornado, big and strong!

**Jack Healy  (8)**
**Portway Junior School**

# Bombing!

This is my poem, about the tragic bombing!

The deafening sounds of children crying in the night
It goes on all day in the light

German bombers, bombing London!
When we are trapped in the dungeon

People dying because of the war!
When we're just bounding along!

And that is the end!

**Rachel Suffling (11)**
**Portway Junior School**

# Earthquake

An earthquake is a roar coming from a hungry tiger,
It's black like violent charcoal about to burn,
The earthquake feels like a volcano has erupted,
It's like blood dripping from the Devil's cold eyes,
The earthquake feels like the torture of small helpless children crying
for help,
It tastes cold and wrong like a frozen life!

**Hope Turner (10)**
**Portway Junior School**

# Silence

Silence is white like a polar bear
It sounds like a breeze blowing in the air
It tastes like a mint fresh in your mouth
It smells like freezing water giving you a brain freeze
It feels like a cuddly stuffed dog with loads of hairs
It reminds me of a boring day with nothing to do.

**Liam Williams (10)**
**Portway Junior School**

# What Is Love?

Love is partnership

Love is caring
Kisses are love
Love can be a wedding
Friends give love for you
Sometimes they care for you
And you will never forget me
I am *love*.

**Jade Donnelly  (9)**
Portway Junior School


# Fund-raising

It tastes like chocolate money
It looks kind and happy
It smells like a marinated spare rib
It sounds like money chinking
It feels warm and cuddly
Fund-raising is yellow like a shining sun
It moves like water in a swimming pool.

**Tom Beaton  (10)**
Portway Junior School


# The Earthquake

It's a piece of rubbish
The colour of dirt
It looks all crumbly like old rocks
It smells a bit like a bonfire
It sounds all scary and like I'm going to die
It feels all shaky and scary.

**Imogen George  (10)**
Portway Junior School

# A Witch Poem

*(Inspired by 'Macbeth')*

Hubble, bubble, toil and trouble
A toenail from an elephant
The gunk from a bogeyman
The slime from an eyeball
A toe from a dead noseless man

Hubble, bubble, toil and trouble
A mouldy piece of cheese
The legs from a spider!
Half a chopped up worm
The blood from a vampire.

Hubble, bubble, toil and trouble
Hubble, bubble with a stubble.

**Hayley Williamson  (9)**
**Portway Junior School**


# Witches' Spell

*(Inspired by 'Macbeth')*

*Double, double, toil and trouble*
*Fire burn and cauldron bubble*
As these gruesome words are spoken
This grimy spell can never be broken
Tooth of wolf with a gift, it's the slimy token
Double, double, toil and trouble
Fire, burn and cauldron bubble
We take the adder by its tail
And shake it for some ginger ale
As we do that the poison turns pale
*Double, double, toil and trouble*
*Fire burn and cauldron bubble.*

**Hannah Fretton  (10)**
**Portway Junior School**

# World War II

All that could be seen was
Bombs coming down from the sky.

After all the bombs were dropped they
Looked like splattered pies.

What a bad time all this has been,
For all the people who were in this scene.

All that could be heard was the screeching noises
Of people dying and people in fear
I so wish I was not here.

What a bad time all this has been
For all the people who were in this scene.

All they could feel was the frightening fear inside
And all the people felt that the Germans had lied.

**Chloe Mack  (10)**
**Portway Junior School**


# The Ultimate All-stars

Buffon makes blinding saves
Carvalho crushes attacks
Ferdinand thrashes forwards
Nesta never slacks
Robben is as quick as a bullet
Ronaldinho's raging with skills
Zidane is as old as Elvis
Gerrard hits the ball over hills
Ronaldo is as fat as a rhino
Adriano always scores
Henry hammers hair-raising goals
But Mourinho never bores
And that's the team that always roars.

**Liam Williams (10) and James Pitt  (9)**
**Portway Junior School**

# World War II

Bombs screaming and crashing at the sound of the air raid sirens,
Screeching fire,
Explosions of houses turning into smoke,
Fires crackling in the harsh winter's breeze,
Destruction of London,
Scarred ash under my feet,
The rubble of one great street,
Yesterday this world was the best place on Earth,
Today I wish I was never born.

**Samuel Hunt  (11)**
**Portway Junior School**


# The Tsunami

The tsunami smells of fear, like having a gun pointed at your head.
It feels like a world without anyone to see, to trust.
A tsunami sounds like crashing waves attacking a community.
A tsunami is like the colour red making all people angry.
It looks like the crunching mouth of a shark coming to get you.
It tastes like bitter evil that nature threw at these people.
The tsunami leaves people with nothing
Nothing but devastation.

**Nicola Fletcher  (11)**
**Portway Junior School**


# Fund-raising

Fund-raising sounds like a fairground full of people
It feels like a soft, fluffy puppy dog licking my face
It looks like a child in a care home finally getting adopted
Fund-raising smells like a big ball of candyfloss
It tastes like my favourite sweets, sizzling on my tongue
The colour of fund-raising is deep blue, warming people's hearts.

**Shannon Goy  (11)**
**Portway Junior School**

# Earthquake

It feels rumbly and bumpy from the most serious conditions
It tastes like the most horrible Brussels's sprouts in the world
It smells bad like the most rotten eggs that you could look at and smell
It looks like big rocks that crumble on houses and kill people
It sounds like the grumbling, churning sounds of an army tank
The colours are dark and dull like black
The shape is spiky and edgy
The sight of it is horrific and fiery
That's an *Earthquake*.

**Jack Barrett  (11)**
Portway Junior School


# Tsunami

It sounds like a massive heart beating for those suffering
A tsunami is red because the red Devil's eyes brighten the dark
                                                    gloomy night with anger
It looks like a whole pile of water being swallowed by a plug
It tastes like bitter revenge on the city
It smells like the rubber collapsing off the houses
It gives them devastation and fear like the tear of the first baby born,
                                                    hunger and fear!

**Andrea Kershaw  (10)**
Portway Junior School


# Indonesia

It sounds like a city with people rushing around
It is a calm blue with a pink and yellow horizon
It tastes of the salty ocean and the green melon trees
It looks like a sunny beach with the sun shining all day
It feels like the sandy water is rushing over you
It smells like the coral ocean and the melon trees that stand tall.

**Katie Brown  (11)**
Portway Junior School

# Indonesia!

It sounds like thunder about to strike with lightning
It sounds like a city crashing to the ground.

It feels like someone has died and you are very upset
It feels like a broken leg or arm.

It smells of water and lots of mud.

It looks like a deserted island with nothing there at all
Apart from broken down houses.

It reminds me of when a bomb has hit an island
And everyone has gone.

**Thomas Hunt  (11)**
**Portway Junior School**


# Earthquake!

An earthquake is something that makes the earth shake and rumble
The colour of the earthquake is the colour of red devils
The earthquake sounds like a massive plastic bag when you squeeze it
and it makes a funny noise
It feels like you're being generous and you feel like you're kind
It tastes like a rotten egg and a 200-year-old packet of crisps
It smells like a box full of dead bodies.

**Jamie Batchelor  (11)**
**Portway Junior School**


# Earthquake

It tastes like a fishcake covered in custard
Earthquakes are like a big devil's hole with red flashes of death
                              coming towards them
It looks like big lumps of bad earth just about to burst out in flames
It sounds like loud surround sound booming in your ear
It feels like a rough piece of hard fabric tearing in your ear
It smells like a burnt bonfire that's just been put out.

**Richard Lowe  (10)**
**Portway Junior School**

# Earthquakes!

An earthquake sounds like there is a massive tummy
rumbling over and over
The colour is red like the flag of Turkey and a deep
brown wood of an ancient house's roof
It feels like the Earth is being taken from under my
Feet. It looks like someone is opening
their mouth to have dinner
It smells like the cheese
still being saved from
the First World War
The spurting of lava
looks like the
spurting of food
The spreading
of the crack is nearly as quick as the
spreading of a highly contagious cold!

**Kate Mee  (10)**
**Portway Junior School**


# Fund-Raising

It tastes like chocolate money

It is yellow because
yellow is happy and bright

It looks kind and happy

Fund-raising
It sounds like money        is happy
pouring into a bucket    like a smiley face!

It moves like wind in
the trees

It feels warm and cuddly

It smells like chips with salt and
vinegar.

**Sian Sorensen  (11)**
**Portway Junior School**

# Earthquake Is Coming!

It tastes like a rotten apple that has been in the dustbin since World
War One
It looks like a lighter that has been burnt to bits by a flame-thrower
It feels like a big bit of rough sandpaper being rubbed under your chin
The colour of an earthquake is as red as the Devil's eyes
It sounds like a motorbike going as fast as the fastest car in the world
in a race
It smells like a fire that has just been set alight with petrol in a petrol
station.

**Kieron Dolan  (11)**
**Portway Junior School**


# Fund-raising

It feels like being kind and helpful
It sounds like rustling in the bushes in your back garden
Fund-raising is red and white like the Southampton home kit
It smells like waffles with chocolate sauce on top
It tastes like strawberry doughnuts half-eaten
It looks like my dog, that has just been for a walk.

**Shaun Wilson  (10)**
**Portway Junior School**


# Tsunami

It tastes like muddy water flooding into your mouth
It smells like fear, as if someone is going to stab you
It feels like something is crushing your heart
A tsunami sounds like a dinosaur is taking over the world
A tsunami is red like blood flooding out of a person
It looks like a massive person belly flopping onto the ground
Pain feels like the death of a person.

**Ashley Brown  (10)**
**Portway Junior School**

# Tsunami In Indonesia

Before tsunami!
It feels like the dancing of the golden sun
It reminds me of the glowing silver moon trickling on the ocean
It tastes like a juicy melon flooding your mouth with kindness
It's the colour of Pepsi purple, putting a smile on anyone's face
It sounds like the twittering of sparrows at the crack of dawn
It smells like the sweet daffodils in a sunlit field.

After tsunami!
It's the colour red that lights the Devil's eyes
It sounds like the roaring of a thunderstorm
It feels like the torture of a small helpless child
It reminds me of the cold violence that many suffer
It smells like the coldness of death
It tastes like blood dribbling down your chin.

**Georgia Loftus  (10)**
**Portway Junior School**


# Earthquake

An earthquake is as stealthy as a
lion suddenly pouncing on its prey
It feels like a rough piece of sandpaper
The colour of an earthquake is black like burnt toast
It sounds like a hungry stomach before dinner
It smells like a carton of milk from 1895
It looks like a roaring hurricane in its prime
It tastes like a plate of old mouldy cheese
The flowing lava is a sea of fire
The crack in the ground grows like a cut from scissors.

**Murray Yelf  (11)**
**Portway Junior School**

# Fund-Raising

It tastes like chocolate money
It looks kind and happy
It smells like chips with salt and vinegar
It sounds like money pouring into a bucket
It feels warm and kind
Fund-raising is happiness like a smiley face
It moves like wind in the trees
It's yellow, because yellow is happy
It's red, because red is heart-warming, yet angry
It's pure kindness
And it's sunny like the flag of Macedonia!

**Archie Sturt  (10)**
**Portway Junior School**


# Tsunami

Blue for water crashing
A tsunami is like chocolate
It looks like it is swallowing the city
A tsunami tastes like sea salt and the most worst flavours
It smells like crusty, rusty sea salt
It feels like it is dripping into your hands melting away
It sounds like the people are screaming
For help and mercy
The pain of death and water crashing
On the dead bodies, but feeling nothing
Because they have already felt it.

**Kenneth Gates  (10)**
**Portway Junior School**

# Snowball

S nowballs fly through misty skies
N ight-time snow sprinkles softly down
O ak trees stand stripped and bare
W atery snow melts away
B uses slip and slide on icy roads
A nother Christmas comes upon us
L icking lips sip hot chocolate
L ogs crackle, burn and burst.

**Imogen Savage  (8)**
**Rookesbury Park School**


# Snowmen

S oggy, snowy frosty night
N aughty children throwing snowballs
O utside snow is falling gently
W oolly hats keep your head warm
M aking snowmen, white and fat
E verybody wraps up warm
N umb fingers, cold and tingling.

**Masahiro Nishikawa  (7)**
**Rookesbury Park School**


# Frost

F rosty nights are dark and cold
R osy noses are red like fire
O utside mornings are white with snow
S nowy trees shiver coldly
T rees are bare and frosty.

**Jack Keogh  (7)**
**Rookesbury Park School**

## Autumn Days

Autumn days are chilly and crisp
The trees are bare and full of mist
The nights are dark and very cold
This year's flowers are very old

Fireworks fly in the sky
They pop and bang, way up high
The farmers work so hard all day
While children run outside to play.

**Anna Cooke  (8)**
**Rookesbury Park School**


## Snowmen

S nowball fights make noses bright red
N ight-times are cold and we snuggle in bed
O ld oak trees are covered in sugary snow
W inter ice freezes the water outside
M en chop trees to put in the red glowing fire
E njoying drinking hot chocolate inside
N o one knows when Jack Frost visits.

**Lydie Stephenson  (7)**
**Rookesbury Park School**


## Autumn Days

Autumn leaves turn to red
Woolly hat warms my head
Sparkly fireworks bang and boom
Up in the sky, they zing and zoom.

**Katherine Young  (7)**
**Rookesbury Park School**

# Autumn Days

Autumn lady lays her cloak down
Children come and play from the town
Leaves are orange, golden, red
Woolly hat upon my head

Autumn mornings crisp and cold
Houses lit up, bright and bold
Farmers collecting all the hay
Ready for the harvest day

Outside it is very chilly
Pumpkin faces look so silly
Orange pumpkins glow at night
What a beautiful, calming sight

Glittering fireworks, zoom and zing
Hear them *swish, bang, boom* and *bing.*

**Chloe Pleydell (8)**
**Rookesbury Park School**


# The Hanger

The hanger comes late at night
He likes to give children an awful fright
He drags them by the hair to hang
He sucks their blood through one big fang

He reduces their bones to little crumbs
And when they run for their mums
He rips them up into little bits
And throws them into deep, dark pits

He has one flaming fang that drips with blood
His flat, hairy feet walk with a thud
His golden eyes glow in the dark
Upon you he will leave his mark.

**Alistair Main  (8)**
**Rookesbury Park School**

# Autumn Days

Autumn lays her cloak on the ground
Children come from all around
Rusty gold leaves fall down in the breeze
Children play and slip till they freeze

Whilst children play, *boom, boom, boom!*
The fireworks zoom, zoom, zoom!
Farmers plough the wheat from dawn
In the morn they collect the corn.

**Maddie Falconer  (7)**
**Rookesbury Park School**

# Autumn Days

Warm wrapped up children play in leaves
Cold trees are naked in the breeze
Leaves have been dyed, orange and gold
Autumn colours are bright and bold

Farmers plough on a crispy morn
Working hard from dusk to dawn
Fireworks zoom up into the sky
Banging and booming, way up high.

**Joseph Hawkins  (7)**
**Rookesbury Park School**

# Autumn Days

Golden leaves twist to the ground
While children play and stomp around
Grizzly bears crawl in their caves
When rattling skeletons jump out of their graves

Wheat and hay are tied in a bundle
As people begin to shiver and trundle
Sparkling fireworks burst into flames
While children enjoy their autumn games.

**Beatrix Bates  (9)**
**Rookesbury Park School**

## Autumn Days

Pumpkins shine in the night
Spooky creatures hide from the light
Fireworks twist up in the sky
Zooming around, way up high

Children play in the leaves
Bare trees sway in the breeze
Orange, brown, red and gold
Autumn colours are so bold.

**Hector Butcher (7)**
**Rookesbury Park School**


## Autumn Days

Rusty leaves fall to the ground
As in the breeze trees start to sway
Harvest time has come around
So farmers plough their hay.

Fireworks make a banging sound
Everyone starts to stare
Skeletons come up from the ground
And witches from their lair.

**Rowan Golland (8)**
**Rookesbury Park School**


## Storms

I can hear the loud rain lashing
As on the roof the hail is crashing
Thunder comes down with a *boom!*
Lightning strikes with a *zoom!*
Trees fall down with a *crash*
Windows break with a *smash*.

**Alexander White (8)**
**Rookesbury Park School**

# Autumn Days

Children rush about in the town
As golden leaves come swirling down
Happy children have rushed out to play
On this lovely autumn day.

Bright coloured fireworks zoom and whiz
As witches cauldrons bubble and fizz
As toasty fires warmly glow
Chilly winds start to softly flow.

Farmers plough from dusk to dawn
Oats and barley, wheat and corn
Harvest has left all the fields bare
Crops are gathered up to share.

**Abigail Guy  (9)**
**Rookesbury Park School**


# Remember, Remember

Fantastic fireworks up so high
Rockets almost touch the sky
Catherine wheels spin round and round
Fizzing so low, almost on the ground!

A blazing bonfire burning all night long
Flames crackling loud and strong
People looking around and gazing
Fireworks well and truly amazing.

Sizzling sausages wrapped in a bun
Squirting ketchup is lots of fun!
I love fireworks and Bonfire Night
With the beautiful colours all so bright.

**Camilla Longman  (9)**
**Rookesbury Park School**

# Winter Is Here

Winter is here
Riding on her white horse
Her long snowy hair tumbling
All scared at the sight of her
Her silver gown of sparkling diamonds
Drags behind her
Her ice-blue eyes are cold
Icicles shoot from her fingertips
And they stab to the ground
She stamps her feet
With her silver, shining shoes
Shattering plants with her coldness
She blows sweet kisses to the ponds
Laughing as they turn to ice

Frost burst out of her glistening necklace
Windows shiver as they turn to ice
Animals hide in the warmth
Scared they might freeze.

**Heidi Sidorina  (10)**
**Rookesbury Park School**

# Fireworks

Whirling fire
Flashing light
Shooting stars
Sky so bright

Gold and silver fountains
Brighten up the sky
Crimson, purple, pink and blue
Racing high, off they fly

Sparklers fizz, there's bangs everywhere
Bright lights illuminate the sky
*Fizz, zoom, whoosh*, that is how they go
And there's a bonfire smouldering high.

**Olivia Bowman  (10)**
**Rookesbury Park School**

# Spring's Arrival

She glides through the air
Making everything green, colourful, bright
Water streams down the hills
And fresh water floats
Jumping and dodging round rocks

Her green grassy dress
Opens up the buds
In one swift movement
She sighs in relief
As baby lambs are born
She touches trees with her violet hair
And one by one
The leaves spring into life

The winter storms
Turn into little breezes
With a kick of her blossom slippers
She calls children
Into the seas
And plays with them
Within the waves.

**Kate Falconer  (10)**
**Rookesbury Park School**


# Autumn Days

Golden leaves fall to the ground
While children play all around
Stamping, jumping, crackling and crunching
Steaming pumpkin soup for lunch.

Farmers work to harvest the wheat
When children start to trick or treat
Witches' cauldrons boil and bubble
Little children get into trouble!

**Charlotte Woodhouse  (8)**
**Rookesbury Park School**

# Spring Green

She wakes the ground
After a long night's sleep
Her breath brings life
To the land
Her green dress
Makes the grass grow high

As she skips along
The trees blossom behind her
Flowers spring up
As she kisses each one in turn
Her long flowery hair
Brings sunshine to the sky

The snow melts
As if it is not wanted
The rabbits come out
Of their hiding place
To play with each other
The lambs leap around her
As she trails along the grass.

**Laurence Golland  (10)**
**Rookesbury Park School**


# Summer's Light

Summer in her long golden dress
With flowers in her hair
And grassy cloak
Dragging behind her
Dances through the fields
Laughing sunshine and
Bringing cool breezes
Birds flutter around her
Singing to her tune
Children follow her
Playing in her wake.

**Lauren Norton  (11)**
**Rookesbury Park School**

# Summer Has Started

As summer floats past
The animals appear
She starts to sing
And wakes the sleepy flowers
Who bloom in her light

Her fluttering purple dress
Flows behind
Soft and calm
Her golden sunshine hair
Tumbles gloriously

As summer takes a breath
She turns
And sees a sweet bird singing
She starts to dance
And the birds flit in the breeze.

**Jade Hurley  (10)**
**Rookesbury Park School**


# Autumn Is Upon Us

As autumn walks
The leaves change colour
His golden hair
Sways in the wind
His cloak of brown and yellow
Floats above the flowers
As he strides
The birds change their tune
Trees transform
And hide
In their autumn colours
He whistles and calls upon the wind
To paint his colours on the leaves
And clear the path
To let him through.

**Samuel Earle  (10)**
**Rookesbury Park School**

# The Sense Of Adventure

You can smell it from a mile away
The sense of adventure come to play
With the biggest smile you've ever seen
You never know just where she's been

She climbed the tallest tree one night
Which gave her mother such a fright
She climbed a wall and then jumped down
She's the most adventurous girl around!

She's always in trouble at my school
Jumping into the swimming pool
Forgetting her homework and having food fights
Making big holes in her school tights

But however naughty she's a really good friend
A helping hand she's ready to lend
And if you're bored and wanting to play
The sense of adventure's not far away!

**Philippa Blunden  (10)**
**Rookesbury Park School**


# The Wickedness Of Winter

The snow queen frowns as she peers out
To see red leaves and trees so stout
She strides out of her icy palace
To show the world her cruelty and malice
She stabs the ground with stiletto heels
And freezes anything that appeals
She kisses the flowers with cold black lips
And makes everything die without a blood drip
She sighs with wickedness and a handful of woe
A snowflake falls and it starts to snow
She glides along without making a sound
As her silver gown flows, she freezes the ground
Most vain and wicked is thou art
She's very proud of her cold black heart.

**Alex Chandler  (11)**
**Rookesbury Park School**

# Summer's Here

Her bright yellow hair
Brings light and warmth
To the earth
Her golden dress
Dances along the path behind her
As flowers burst into bloom
Reaching out to her
Summer twirls in happiness
Through the meadows
Butterflies flutter
To her sweet song
And flock to her radiant gifts.

**Emily Benson-Rhodes (11)**
**Rookesbury Park School**

# Freedom

Freedom;
Release from captivity
A spirit that is a rarity
To many people
A feeling, some have never witnessed
An experience some will never encounter
An immortal soul.

**Joseph Scandrett (9)**
**Rucstall Primary School**

# Bullies

Bully pretends he is hard and tough
Bully has no friends whatsoever
Bully is selfish and mean
Bully is actually frightened on the inside.

**Jack Verling (9)**
**Rucstall Primary School**

# Freedom

Freedom is nature, scattered all around the earth
Freedom means cloudless skies
Freedom is fragile little droplets, falling from trees
Freedom means wisdom, exploring the future.

Freedom is a fountain of learning
Freedom means power in your soul
Freedom is a huge pattern of rain
Freedom means extraordinary things are about to begin.

**Paige Hollis  (8)**
**Rucstall Primary School**


# Friendship

A friend is . . .
Someone who smiles at you
Shares a secret with you
Looks after you when someone has hurt your feelings
Someone who cares for you
Shares toys and plays with you
They are always beside you
To pick you up when you have fallen over.

**Lauren Kelly  (9)**
**Rucstall Primary School**


# Friends

A friend
Shares your secrets
Never leaves you alone
Someone who picks you off your feet
And cares.

**Christy Paul  (9)**
**Rucstall Primary School**

# Rivalry

Rivalry presents fiery-red
Provoking vulnerable opponents
Conquering foolish minds
Who dares to challenge them
Rivalry troops facing blistering forces
Devoted to the task afoot
It becomes accustomed to armies retreating
Alliances called
Rivalry penetrates preserved souls of love
It lurks in demented corners
Consuming glory passing opportunities
To snatch up the real prize
Friends!

**Alexander Goodall  (11)**
**Rucstall Primary School**


# Freedom

Freedom is a privilege to all who use it
Freedom is a power, when used correctly
Freedom is a free rein to do what you want
Freedom is an opportunity to be responsible
Freedom is like a bird running free.

**Reece Chapman  (10)**
**Rucstall Primary School**


# Freedom

Freedom is a powerful thing that you can't touch, eat or smell
Freedom is like someone from jail running free
Freedom is a decision that chooses who you play with
Freedom is a thing that sets you free.

**Emma-Louise McCarthy  (9)**
**Rucstall Primary School**

# Stress

I'm yellow
My tough sides lingering too
The limit
I'm the one who smashes your marriage
Taking you on journeys
Through versions of Hell
I stop your life's joyful ways
Compelling you to destroy your beloved treasures
I'm like a rollercoaster that never stops
Destroying you in phases of
*Darkness*
I push people to the brink
Forcing them in amongst
Problems from which they cannot escape.

**Adam Gough  (11)**
**Rucstall Primary School**


# Love

Pink, fluffy, heart-shaped
I hug when storm clouds gather
Short, quite, calm
I never lose my temper
Happy days I bring
Safety, trust
I come to you when no one's there
I'm your guiding hand
Making your spirits rise
Love I am
My presence will bring eternal sunrise.

**Amy Jones  (10)**
**Rucstall Primary School**

# Bullying

A bully is
Small inside, but thinks he is big
A bully is a clone of a devil
A bully is jealous
Small
Shameless
Atrocious
Wrong
Vicious
Foul
Mean
The victim of bullying is in for a treat. *Not!*

**Matthew Goodall  (9)**
**Rucstall Primary School**


# Embarrassment

I hide
Stage frightened
Hiding behind opaque shields
Despairing
Hating spotlights
Keeping back
Panic increases
Fame's a different person
I give others confidence
I disappear when audience participation is needed
I am not the stand out flame
I am the coal left behind.

**Christopher Rolfe  (10)**
**Rucstall Primary School**

# Rivalry!

I'm a steamy grey shade of competiveness
You run, I sprint faster
You score one, I'll score two
You paint a picture, I'll paint a masterpiece
You lose, I'll win
I ruin your dreams, I don't care about you
I only care about my reputation
I'm the best at everything
My venomous deeds poison people's minds to provoke each other
*Aggressively!*

**Lewis Greenhalf  (11)**
**Rucstall Primary School**


# We Will Remember

We will remember the great soldier he was
We will remember how he was fighting to keep people alive
We will remember how brave he was and how great a friend he was
We will remember how he protects each other
We will remember how supportive and accurate he was to fight.

**Samantha Coulbeck  (10)**
**Rucstall Primary School**


# Freedom

Freedom is the maker of stars
It takes animals out of cages
Freedom allows me round my friends' houses
It separates country from country
Freedom lets baby robins out of their eggs.

**Cavan Reid  (8)**
**Rucstall Primary School**

# Loneliness

Loneliness sits in the corner in a box
Trapped
Always in the dark
It waits for someone who never comes
It whispers:
'I am invisible, nobody notices me.'
A transparent shadow against the wall
Loneliness empties your heart
To leave it cold and hard like a stone
He wonders if he will ever be free?

**Stephanie Rounce  (10)**
**Rucstall Primary School**


# Love

Love is soft and melting as chocolate
A jigsaw of tears and laughter
It's red heart pumps blood, warm, tingly
Love is a companion who knows how to talk without words
A comforting blanket wraps itself around you
Love is the key to a box of happiness.

**Emily West  (10)**
**Rucstall Primary School**


# Joy

Joy floats like a bubble
Blue as a summer sky
Light and airy as it lands on you
Fizzes you up like a bottle of champagne
It laughs and smiles but never frowns
Joy fights anger and puts it in the dump.

**Naomi Cole  (10)**
**Rucstall Primary School**

# Jealousy

Want stains my blackened heart
With a glare so deadly
It cuts deep into infected skin.

Those with better
Have worse to fear
As jealousy walks in their shadow.

Controlled by its yearning
To have the divine
Jealousy endures for this day

His hatred conjures
A deadly impact
He will never surrender.

He tortures you
Until the end
What happens next?
Who knows?

**Ruhee Padhiar  (11)**
**Rucstall Primary School**


# Fear

Orange, purple - spotted ever-shaking
I'm one who never stops hiding
I'm one with no hope at all
I'm one who never seeks courage
Courage: my enemy
Fear: my power
I'm one that will never leave you
I'm here until you overcome your fear.

**Michael Paul  (11)**
**Rucstall Primary School**

# Sadness

Sadness is scared
It is worried
Sadness is afraid
Frightened, of everything
Wishing he was someone else
Sadness has no power
He is a slave
It is always in his corner
Sadness has no friends
He is always hiding
Sadness is always picked last
He is a coward
Sadness is the opposite of happiness
Other people think they are big whilst making him feel small
Sadness is always
*Alone.*

**Greg Donaldson  (11)**
**Rucstall Primary School**


# Temptation

Temptation is against the human body
It makes you want things, that you know you mustn't and break things
It is black with a minute lightning streak down its left cheek
Temptation has a grimace like no other
It will overpower even the strongest minds
It makes you want to steal
Temptation is rarely a wonderful thing
Exquisite intelligence overcomes it
Sometimes
But can you?

**Conor Reid  (10)**
**Rucstall Primary School**

# Worry!

Worry . . .
Is green with: illness, fever, exhaustion
Beside myself with fear of my every single action
Money, family
I'm trapped, I can't escape, I feel lonely
What should I do?
Where should I go?
What will happen to me?
Breaking body parts
Crumbling bones
Trembling with fear of . . . everything . . .
That I do not understand!
It's evil for you
But sometimes I wish I could . . .
*Disappear!*

**Joshua Kinderman (11)**
**Rucstall Primary School**


# Friendship

Friendship's two-faced
Friendship's yellow
Warm, cosy
You can face elements
Never alone
You become jolly
Face like the sun
But . . .
Betrayal starts to happen
Pain as well as peace
The pain never-ending
Frustration gathers
The pain never-ending
Friendship's two-faced.

**Holly Linehan (11)**
**Rucstall Primary School**

# Despair

I'm grey and I have no hope left inside
I float like a grey cloud in isolation
I'm like a leech that feeds on courage
I walk around with no sense of direction
Disappointment is my friend
Courage is my foe
I make people give in and I make them groan
Like snow melting in springtime sun
Wherever I go the rain seems to follow.

**Luke Stratton  (10)**
**Rucstall Primary School**

# Waves

Boiling hot
Sun shining bright
Like a diamond reflecting in the light.
Children playing
Like cowboys saying,
'Howdee pardner'
Laughing crazy.

Crashing
Smashing
Like a lion roaring for its prey
Racing
Screaming
Like a stampede
Finding a safe place.

Shocked
Worried
Finding their houses below them.
Wail, weep
No food or water
For the rest of the week.

**Amy Brockway  (11)**
**St Paul's Catholic Primary School, Portsmouth**

# Waves

Towering like a ton of bricks,
The earth crashed down.
People sat in despair waiting for bad news,
As the tsunami cascaded more dead bodies.
Waves of thunder destroyed all in sight
And played with people's minds.
Suddenly, hope grew in their hearts,
Money was given to buy food and water,
Shelters were built and still are.

**Ebony Adolphe  (11)**
**St Paul's Catholic Primary School, Portsmouth**


# Tsunami

Rushing through the enormous wave as it cascaded down,
Like an angry giant jumping up and down.

Waves of grief ruined Christmas for everyone,
By separating families apart,
Like somebody stealing presents from everyone's homes.

Waves of grief killed thousands of people,
Like somebody lost and never found.

**Jayne Cummings  (11)**
**St Paul's Catholic Primary School, Portsmouth**


# The River

The river is spinning like a professional ballet dancer,
Performing a pirouette.
Sparkling, like admiring stars in the baby-blue sky.
Splashing like a toddler in the bath.
Bubbling like roasting boiled water.
The river crashes against hard rocks.

**Ellie-Louise Brown  (10)**
**St Paul's Catholic Primary School, Portsmouth**

# Silent Killer

On Boxing Day, a killer wave
Was thrashing, crashing, bashing, houses down.

Thumping, bumping, powering through,
As people were swept into the raging tsunami,
Whack, bang, smack, as houses fall,
There is nothing left.

The day after Christmas,
Oh how cold, dark and alone they must be
And what about their families?
Cold, lifeless and dead,
They must be crying right now.

Let's give money so they can build
And not be killed
By yet another tsunami.

So he does not sigh
But he will still
Be crying in the place
It struck.

**Jamie Francalanza  (10)**
St Paul's Catholic Primary School, Portsmouth


# The River

The fish dart through the sapphire stream,
In and out of the bottle-green weed,
Until they reach the cliff's edge.
The waterfall approaches,
The water thunders down,
Like a curtain falling into foam.
Now the river slows,
Hissing like a snake
And ends its journey,
As a still pond.

**Sarrah Agulan  (10)**
St Paul's Catholic Primary School, Portsmouth

# River

As blue as the heavens,
Twirling like water spiralling down the plughole,
Like a sparkling ribbon on the dressing table.
It sounds like a human splashing in the pool,
Sparkling like a diamond surround.
Moving as quickly as thunder,
Like a snake weaving through trees,
Like a toddler splashing, learning to swim,
Like a ballet dancer twirling.

**Nicole Sainty (10)**
**St Paul's Catholic Primary School, Portsmouth**


# River

Rushing like excited children late for school.
Winding and twirling into classes.
Shimmering and shivering
Like shiny goldfish looking for food.
Sparkling like stars
Dazzling above clear blue water,
Reflecting . . .

**Josh Duff, Alfie Gawn & Danny Mooney (10)**
**St Paul's Catholic Primary School, Portsmouth**


# The River

Splashing like an infant bouncing lively in a puddle,
Swirling like a slimy sticky snake,
Twisting like a spiral piece of pasta,
Bumpy like a solid rock,
Twirling like a ballerina spinning,
Rushing like you're late for school,
Spitting like a ferocious camel,
Bubbling like boiling hot lava.

**Hollie Jeans (10)**
**St Paul's Catholic Primary School, Portsmouth**

# Seaside

When I go to the seaside,
I can hear the waves roaring like sea lions,
When my feet touch the water
I feel safe and calm.

I can swim too,
I jump off the rocks into the sea,
My dad says I look like a mermaid
Wiggling my feet
I wish I was a mermaid
I wish I could live in the sea.

Then I get an ice cream
It tastes lovely in my mouth
When it's cold and the day's hot,
My mum asks me why I love the sea
I say, because it looks so peaceful
And so strong
I love whirlpools
So that's why I love the sea.

**Rosalind Waite  (10)**
**St Paul's Catholic Primary School, Portsmouth**


# The River

Thrashing as if it was late for work,
The river strikes through the forest,
Meandering like a ribbon just about to be tied in a bow,
The river is tranquil now, glittering like smashed glass,
It twinkles in the roasting midday sun,
The calmness is almost over now, the waterfall is nearing,
Swirling like the wind, the river picks up speed,
Tumbling and cascading as if in a tantrum,
Rapidly plunging towards the rocks below,
*Crash!* A grand entrance into a pool of serenity,
The journey has ended.

**Carmen Langworthy  (11)**
**St Paul's Catholic Primary School, Portsmouth**

# The Waves

Crashing against the palm trees
They got bigger and bigger.
Wiping out everything in its path
Getting more powerful as the time goes by.

People running as fast as they could
Knowing that if they don't
They will be washed away
The memories that they have had
Have been destroyed in front of their faces.

People feel sorry for them,
But are glad it wasn't them.
People give and give,
But they can't change how they feel.

**Scarlett Robinson (10)**
**St Paul's Catholic Primary School, Portsmouth**


# The River

Darting like vibrant red blood through your head,
Meandering as if you were in a coiled, isolated maze,
Glistening like a transparent contact lens,
Slashing as if you were in a ship when a storm has occurred,
Spiralling like a colossal tornado,
Revolving like you're speeding around an eternal roundabout.

Crashing violently like a herd of stampeding elephants,
Scintillating like a lucid chandelier,
Convoluting like a writhing serpent,
Flowing rapidly into the bottomless, vast ocean.

**Sean Burby (11)**
**St Paul's Catholic Primary School, Portsmouth**

# Shocking Tsunami

The wall of water and terror,
Bulldozing hotels, houses and shopping centres.
No one knew it was coming,
No warning system.
Governments didn't think it would happen there.
No superheroes to save them.
Batman, Superman, Spider-Man . . .
None of them real.
Devastation.
Countries, rivals, enemies reunite to help.
Food, water, paramedics and overall help
Arrives by transport such as helicopters, ships, delivering goods.
Thank technology for giving us what it has.

**Callum Veale  (10)**
**St Paul's Catholic Primary School, Portsmouth**


# Waves

Silent as a tiger,
The wave came to destroy.
Everything in its way
Was soon to be nothing.
It left waves of despair,
It left waves of grief.
Many people's lives were taken,
Constant supplies are being sent
From all over the world.
Constant waves of compassion,
Now all that's left to do
Is hope for the people who lived.

**Paul Hooper  (11)**
**St Paul's Catholic Primary School, Portsmouth**

# Waves

Waves of destruction,
A spiteful and ugly being,
Like a wall of water wiping out everything in its path.

Crashing down,
Everywhere is enveloped in screams,
A selfish hooligan.

Nothing can stop it,
It's like a powerful, greedy man just wanting to make money,
But in this case, trying to kill and destroy,
It is like Hell.

Waves of despair,
Weeping humans crying for their dead families,
Imagine having nothing,
No food, no water, no shelter, no parents,
Nothing, nothing, nothing . . .
It's all gone.

Waves of grief,
Bodies everywhere,
Most are dead.

Praying for a new beginning,
But it's not coming . . .
Not yet . . .

**Lucy-Ann Catterall  (10)**
**St Paul's Catholic Primary School, Portsmouth**


# Senses

I could hear the waves crashing together.
I could see the fluttering flags with their colourful streamers.
I could feel the wishing wind rising and blowing into the air.
I could smell the gunpowder smoke rising in the sky.
I could taste the stinging of the salty water.

**Molly Jackson  (7)**
**St Paul's Catholic Primary School, Portsmouth**

# Sea Life

Rushing in again and again,
Goes the sea through sun or rain,
But then as winter comes around,
It turns a very ugly brown,
Then cold days pass quickly by,
As the clouds pass over the tide.

The sea has power over all,
As angry as an upset bull,
The sea washes in and out,
Sweeping all left over things about,
Lashing at the fighting fish,
Swishing at the passing mist.

You hear the waves hitting your head,
The angry sea lies upon its bed,
Outraged dogs chase about,
The fun starts when the sun is out,
Salty whirlpools chase round boats,
Rubber dinghies tossed around float.

But when summer comes the fun begins,
So that is when I go to the beach again!

**Eleanor Ransford  (9)**
**St Paul's Catholic Primary School, Portsmouth**


# Waves

Crashing down like a sobbing, spiteful child,
Escaping from a towering, tormenting wall of water,
Destroying everything it could get its hands on,
A nightmare that would never end,
Trying to get away from a never-ending cascading wave,
Running and screaming as if chased by a lion,
Silently, despair grew in their hearts,
Caring like no one cared before,
But it's not coming,
Not yet!

**Shannon Hadley  (10)**
**St Paul's Catholic Primary School, Portsmouth**

# The Terrible Tsunami

Waves slowing building up higher and higher
Crashing and bashing against the sand
Birds flew inland
Then a great, huge wave
Struck
Obviously, the dead people didn't have much luck.

After many victims had died
Thousands of people cried
Still many are missing
People keep on wishing
Countries are raising
God's praising.

**Oliver Hudson  (10)**
**St Paul's Catholic Primary School, Portsmouth**


# Rage

The raging river raced through the mountain
Without a care in the world.
Shooting out of springs like fountains,
Then bumping into rocks as it curled,
Twisting like the unborn child
Whipping its mother, the land.
Shooting the birds in the wild,
Shouting like a normal man.
Jumping, twisting, round and round,
Then as it comes to the valley
It starts to calm down.

**Jessica Jarvis  (11)**
**St Paul's Catholic Primary School, Portsmouth**

# Wave Of Terror . . .

Sunny day
Laughter and play
Nice trees swaying in the breeze
And swirling seas
Reflecting on everyone.

Then suddenly
Bashing and crashing against the sea
Rock
Non-stop.

Screaming
Crying
Dying
Everywhere.

**Liam Kelleher (10)**
**St Paul's Catholic Primary School, Portsmouth**


# The Terrible Disaster

Calm sea
Lovely swaying palm trees
And people laughing
Happy as can be
Sandy beach where people build sandcastles

Crashing and bashing onto the rocks
Sea groaning at people all around
People running for their lives
The crowd shocked and terrified
Charities raising money
As the waves flood the land.

**Daisy Beck (10)**
**St Paul's Catholic Primary School, Portsmouth**

# The Wave

It crashed
And bashed
Made lots of death
It was making people
Take their *last*
Breath!

Depression
And worry went around
The world
Sorrow
And sadness began to
Swirl.

When the news
Finally got out
People were shocked
And started to
*Shout!*

The only colours
People saw
Were black, white and blue
People were upset
And very sorry
But they didn't have a clue.

Spending money
And giving aid
People tried to help
Will this horror
Ever end?
That's what I'm worried about.

**Elisha Pilmoor  (11)**
**St Paul's Catholic Primary School, Portsmouth**

# The Waves

Sun shining
A paradise place
Trees swaying
In the breeze
Children laughing
Having fun
Sea calm
Not for long

Sea is smashing
Sand is gone
I wonder where?
People taken
By the sea
Please come back
Please, please
Come back

I'm so happy
It wasn't mine
Why did it happen, God?
Why? Why? Why?
Please help them
Please, please
We must help them.

**Billy Griffiths  (10)**
**St Paul's Catholic Primary School, Portsmouth**

# Tsunami

I could sense the waves coming towards me
I saw the boats tipping up and down
*tsunami*
I shouted but no one listened
Loads of people died
I was put into hospital.

**Connor Jones  (9)**
**St Paul's Catholic Primary School, Portsmouth**

# Wave

Beautiful day on the beach
Swaying palm trees everywhere
Playing games
Without care
The water clear
The sun shining on the trees.

Crashing
Screaming
People climbing up trees
The wave is coming
People start running
Yelling
Weeping
The wave is pulling people into the ocean
Pushing them out when drowning.

People sobbing
Houses
Buildings destroyed
Countries flooded
Millions homeless
Sadness filling the air
No food
Water
Anywhere.

As people think about this disaster
They say, 'I'm glad me and my family weren't there.'

**Jessica Campbell (10)**
**St Paul's Catholic Primary School, Portsmouth**

# Waves

On holiday, in the sun,
Laughing, talking, shouting,
Palm trees swaying in the breeze,
Everybody is having fun,
Sandy, yellow-golden beaches,
A calm, turquoise sea.

Suddenly, the wave of death,
Crashes down on the island,
Screaming, shrieking, wailing,
People running, people sprinting,
Water covering everything,
A rough, choppy sea wipes out some of the human race.

People are dead,
Crying, weeping, grieving,
Mums, dads, sisters, brothers,
Gone,
Did they deserve it,
Could God let this happen?

Starting from a small amount,
The other countries gave,
Some aid and some money,
Because of the big wave,
The donation soon got bigger,
Then people started to pray,
For the wave that happened,
On Boxing Day.

**Molly Hover  (10)**
**St Paul's Catholic Primary School, Portsmouth**

# Tsunami Strike

The terrible wave came through the night
Crashing, smashing with all its might
Collecting all the sea on its way
The fishes had to swim away.

People running, people crying
Parents were defiantly lying
The wave roaring
The people calling
'Tsunami.'

It came crashing down
The king, I think, lost his crown
He didn't protect his people's lives
Lots, have very sadly died.

The aid is here
It's come to clear
All our bad thoughts
To stop their destruction
And to rebuild their lives.

It has come to heal
Destroy bad health
Help the poor
And bring back the law.

**James Norris  (10)**
**St Paul's Catholic Primary School, Portsmouth**

# On A Boxing Day

At the seaside on a sunny day
Boats out at sea catching fish
Playing in sand, climbing trees, having fun
Swaying trees, calm wind.

Huge waves, buildings destroyed.
Dying. Clashing sounds and covered land.
Swirling sea, blowing wind.
Boats seen crashed on land. Buildings.
Rubble. People dying, crying.

Death toll up, people grieving
Children lost, people found lying
Dead on ground. All around, up and down
Very rarely buildings standing.

People afar and people near, help and help
Because they care. People from
All over pray for them
Because they care enough.
The wave of understanding and caring
Was the last wave for them.

The last quake was today. Hit
An island of innocence that had
Already been hit. Surrounded by mist
And swallowed by water.

**Neil Hayden  (10)**
**St Paul's Catholic Primary School, Portsmouth**

# Tsunami

The tsunami wave caused us grief
Although it was only brief
It made us cry and feel despair
To leave the people much to repair.

The suffering is great
The death we hate
The people left living
Need us to be giving.

All the aid that we post
Goes to the people that need it most
The little children with no mums or dads
Are now feeling terribly sad.

Now is the time to give, give, give,
To allow these children to live.

**George Rogers  (11)**
**St Paul's Catholic Primary School, Portsmouth**


# The Angry Sea

The sea is very noisy,
Crash, roar, swish, goes the sea,
The sea is very dangerous,
Insulting, rough and terrifying.

The waves are strong,
Like an upset bull,
The tsunami shipwrecks the ships,
Down into the sea they go.

The sea is terrifying,
It takes boats from the shore,
The big waves are deadly,
*Whoosh, bang, crush*, goes the sea.

**Tanya Bee  (10)**
**St Paul's Catholic Primary School, Portsmouth**

# Waves

People filled with laughter
Sea bright blue
Everyone playing
Shining sand on the floor
Water shining
Sparkling water
Wonderful day
Trees moving to the breeze
Until the sea goes rough
Birds screeching as they
Scurry away
And then people running
As a huge tsunami is
Coming.
All the racket
Of birds
They all thought the world was over
And then came the tsunami
The tsunami ended
Disaster
Buildings destroyed
People limping and crying
Homes devastated
People homeless
Disaster in Indonesia.

**Christopher Thompson (10)**
**St Paul's Catholic Primary School, Portsmouth**


# My Senses

I could hear factories working.
I could see cloudy skies.
I could feel rusty railings.
I could taste smoke from the chimneys.
I could smell misty, black smoke.

**Erin Blake (8)**
**St Paul's Catholic Primary School, Portsmouth**

# Waves

With my family, having fun
On the beach, nice and calm
Gleaming water, sparkling sand
All the boats catching cod
Peaceful breeze, still and warm
Palm trees swaying, like a dream.

Screaming people running for their lives
Hopes and dreams traumatised
Markets, shops all collapsing
Villagers hiding from the wave,
Panicking animals leaving the city
Finally it's over; not many living.

Tears spreading from house to house,
Like a terrible disease.
Prayers for everyone missing
In the disaster.
Happiness gone, turned into sorrow.

Fund-raiser, charity owner
All giving money
Mums and dads relieved
For their families
Nations caring a lot for others.

**Elliot Salter  (10)**
**St Paul's Catholic Primary School, Portsmouth**


# Monday's Child

Monday's child's name is Ben.
Tuesday's child likes living in a den.
Wednesday's child likes to bake.
Thursday's child does not fake.
Friday's child like to make.
Saturday's child was born in a lake.
But the child that was born on the Sabbath Day
Fights the knights and likes to play.

**Kevin Vandabona  (7)**
**St Paul's Catholic Primary School, Portsmouth**

# A Sea

The sea was really mad,
The salty water rippling around,
Its great, turquoise waves crashing,
It made a rough, roaring sound.

As the sea went on in outrage,
The massive waves kept crashing,
A massive storm broke out,
With very loud splashing.

It was a rocky storm
With whirlpools whirling,
With twisters clashing,
It was like two dangerous fish fighting.

Now the sea is dark blue,
From all its outrage,
It's hammering and swishing has slowed down,
All it makes is a small, swishing sound.

**Scarlett Johnson  (10)**
**St Paul's Catholic Primary School, Portsmouth**


# The Sea

The sea is like
An angry bull raging to the shore
It's powerful and fast
When it hits the rocks, they roar.

The sea is
Rough and dangerous
Bashing and clashing while he says,
'I am the sea! I am the sea!'

Here is a wave
A big one, in fact
There it goes up, then it goes down
And that's how waves disappear into the sand.

**Rachel Herriott  (10)**
**St Paul's Catholic Primary School, Portsmouth**

# Tsunami

Playing children
Golden beach
Glittering sand
Swaying palm trees
Happy.

Crashing waves
Scared children
Black beach
Sand
Broken palm trees
Angry.

Waves gone
Crying children
Deserted beach
Dead sand
Palm trees no more
Sorrow.

Waves settled
Helping children
Busy beach
Glistening sand.

**Joshua Creed  (11)**
**St Paul's Catholic Primary School, Portsmouth**


# Monday's Child

Monday's child is as good as gold.
Tuesday's child never did what he was told.
Wednesday's child always brushes his teeth.
Thursday's child thought south was east.
Friday's child won a trophy today.
Saturday's child just wants to play.
But the child that was born on the Sabbath Day
Reads, teases and hits all day.

**Nicole Crosbourne  (7)**
**St Paul's Catholic Primary School, Portsmouth**

# Wave Of Suffering

Warm morning.
Soothing music
Hot sand
And no breeze.

Wave comes.
No peace
Destruction attacks
And shouting begins.

Peace is shattered.
Sobbing starts
Futures vanquished
Islands gone.

Whispering sea
And calm ocean.
The worrying ends
And the crying begins.

Money rolls in.
Help comes
Silence comes next
And grieving is after.

**Samuel Rogers  (10)**
**St Paul's Catholic Primary School, Portsmouth**


# Waves

The waves were crashing
Bashing and dashing
Destroying everything in its path.
Ruining the earth
I will not laugh.

Depressing badness
Worry and sadness
People crying
And painfully dying.

**Jamie Sharpe  (10)**
**St Paul's Catholic Primary School, Portsmouth**

# Angry Sea

The sea is like
A bull that is upset,
A stormy night in winter,
A roaring lion.

The waves are like
A racing car in a race,
A terrifying twister,
A massive mountain growing,
Bigger and bigger every minute.

The little animals in the sea
Going round and round in a whirlpool,
When the sea is angry.

The sea is like
A bull that is upset,
A stormy night in winter,
A roaring lion.

**Charlotte Smith  (10)**
**St Paul's Catholic Primary School, Portsmouth**


# The Angry Sea

The sea can be very dangerous,
It's rough, powerful, mean and deadly,
It's very deadly when it's stormy.

The waves are very strong,
The waves can last very long,
The sea is like an upset bull.

The waves crash together noisily,
Smashing waves together roughly,
The sea is so deadly.

People say there's a sea monster,
They say it's a giant lobster,
But I think it's just an angry sea.

**Kimberley Malson  (9)**
**St Paul's Catholic Primary School, Portsmouth**

# Bonfire Night

There they are, in the sky,
They are really, really high.

The night before Bonfire Night,
I had a dreadful fright,
That I would see fireworks tonight,
It was fizzing, whizzing,
My drink was fizzing,
I was cringing,
I was singing.

It was dark in the sky,
It wanted to fly,
Boom! Amazing,
I have never seen a sight!

**James Ward-Prowse  (10)**
St Paul's Catholic Primary School, Portsmouth


# Fireworks

Fireworks are colourful,
Coming in all different shapes and sizes.
Bright and shining in the night sky,
Giving you entertainment all night long.

Fireworks are noisy,
Lots of bangs, crashes and booms.
Whiz, whoosh, fizz, crackle,
Loud noises in your ears.

Fireworks turning this way and that,
Zooming through the sky.
Turning speedily,
Whizzing very fast.

**Faith Davies  (10)**
St Paul's Catholic Primary School, Portsmouth

# Bonfire Night

At night I heard a *bang!*
I looked out, it was Bonfire Night.
I watched the rockets soaring,
I saw Catherine wheels spinning,
I stared for as long as it all shone.
The light was amazing,
I just wish I could see them forever.

For so long I watched a lot of reds and greens,
I wish I was a firework,
I would shoot up and explode *bang!*
Out comes red, green, scarlet and blue,
I think it's fantastic.
Then I hear a screeching!
I saw a white thing whizzing!
But now it's faded, it has gone till next time.

**Adam Wilkes (10)**
**St Paul's Catholic Primary School, Portsmouth**


# Bonfire Night

Crackle, crackle,
Booming, booming,
Zooming, zooming,
What is it going to be?

Whooshing rockets,
Sparkling sparklers,
Do you know what it's going to be?

Every rocket's very loud and also screamers too.
Watching the fireworks on the hill,
Watching them go up in pretty patterns.

We love Bonfire Night!

**Yasmine Hayward (10)**
**St Paul's Catholic Primary School, Portsmouth**

# Bonfire Night

I hear a firework
I do, I do
I'm sure I hear a firework
Yes, I do
I did hear a firework.

Did you hear a firework?
Yes, I did, I'm sure of it
A firework is nice in the night.

I smell a bonfire, I do, I do
It comes from next door
Look, look, I do smell a bonfire.

I'm going to a firework party
I see rockets whizzing
It's coming, I'd better move away
Yes, yes, I do have to move away
Unless I want to be burnt.

**Roxanne Hoare  (9)**
**St Paul's Catholic Primary School, Portsmouth**


# Bonfire Night

Bangs from fireworks up so high,
On a really high building, might go boom!
Never go out or they might catch you,
Fireworks dazzling,
In the sky, fire will fly,
Rattlesnakes in the air,
Eliminate the sky,
Night-time fires,
Independent lights,
Grumbling sounds today, oh yeah,
High in the air tonight,
Their colours are bright on every night.

**Martin Davies-Parker  (9)**
**St Paul's Catholic Primary School, Portsmouth**

# Tsunami

A big wave crashed down.
I felt frightened and worried.
The wave came, came down and crushed the houses.
I felt so unhappy and angry, I even felt cross.
I heard people drowning, even beeping horns.
I heard cars driving far, far away.
I heard people shouting, help, help.
It was so strong, people hugged each other, hoping for a miracle.
People praying and shouting.
It looked massive, or even gigantic, or scary, or horrible, I would say.
It killed thousands of people
And washed their bodies away.

A man came out to say,
'Stop you wave, go back to the sea.
You have no right to be here.
Go back into the sea.
Be gone.'
It was over.
*Hooray.*

**Connor Mooney (9)**
**St Paul's Catholic Primary School, Portsmouth**


# Seaside

I am in the water, *splash, splash, splash*
I am going into the crashing, crashing waves, deep, deep, deep
I am in my boat about to go into the deadly, deadly sea
I am in the rushing, rushing waves
I am beginning to get scared as I am entering the rushing,

                                                    rushing waves
I am now in the reef, reef, reef
I am out of the reef, but I am now in twirling water, water, water
I am now getting dragged, dragged down.

**Tyler Dutson (10)**
**St Paul's Catholic Primary School, Portsmouth**

# Tsunami

When the tsunami came, I was horrified
And all of my family was terrified.
People were scared and screaming for help!
Dead fish, dead people, all things floating about!
All kinds of people are really sad
And some people are quite mad.

Tsunami, tsunami, go away,
Tsunami, tsunami, on this beautiful day.

I heard a crack of light,
I heard it in the night.
The boats crashing
And water splashing.
Families all crying,
Loads of people dying.

Tsunami, tsunami, go away,
Tsunami, tsunami, on this beautiful day.

**Millie Manchip (9)**
**St Paul's Catholic Primary School, Portsmouth**


# Fear, Fear, Fear

Fear, fear, fear, the angry sea is near
Storm, storm, storm, it's never very warm
Rain, rain, rain, its storm has regained
Shore, shore, shore, the sea power is never very poor
Dash, dash, dash, lightning starts in a flash.

Crash, crash, crash, the sea clashes with the shore
Bash, bash, bash, the thunder's there in a flash
Roar, roar, roar, the sea lashes against the shore.

**Charlie Cooper (10)**
**St Paul's Catholic Primary School, Portsmouth**

# Tsunami

A huge, crashing wave is what I saw,
Cute, little animals that I adore,
People shouting, screaming for help,
Dead bodies, dead fish, floating about.
When I saw the tsunami, I knew it was bad,
Lots of lost families and people that are sad.

I felt really scared when I saw it coming,
I felt really terrified and all was so cunning,
I felt like I was going to die,
But I could not be a little sly.

All I could hear was screaming voices,
Things smashing and falling off walls,
The tsunami I saw was a big disaster,
It was coming towards me faster and faster.
My parents and me were as frightened as could be,
All of my family were scared, just like me.

**Emma Tolhurst (10)**
**St Paul's Catholic Primary School, Portsmouth**


# Firework Night

On firework night, tonight what can I hear?
I hear banging and crackling and whizzing.

On firework night, tonight what can I see?
I see bright ones and plain ones and gold.

On firework night, tonight what can I feel?
I feel the vibration of the fireworks going off.

On firework night, tonight I'm having fun all right.

**Natasha Merriman (10)**
**St Paul's Catholic Primary School, Portsmouth**

# Tsunami

I would see the sharks flying through the sky
'Cause of the tsunami
People dying, people praying
And bodies floating away
From the wall of water.

The sad people with no homes
Blood is everywhere
What can we do?
People want to be happy
But they are unhappy
With homes destroyed
Why God, why?

The bodies are floating away
The wall of water traps us
The tsunami kills us
People are dying
Please save us
I do not want to die.

**Alex Palmer  (9)**
**St Paul's Catholic Primary School, Portsmouth**


# Bonfire Night

Rockets are blasting, making a bang,
Did you hear it? I did I am sure of it.

Catherine wheels whizzing round and round
Did you see the sparks? I did, I did.

What's now? Diamond showers
Oh, look at the colours
Did you see it?
*I did!*

**Tenaya Riddell  (10)**
**St Paul's Catholic Primary School, Portsmouth**

# Tsunami

I was frightened,
Of the enormous wave,
Screams and shouts,
From the people around.

I chose to run,
I hurried, I did,
I thought I would die,
Along with the sharks and fish.

I heard something huge coming closer towards me,
I could hear the enormous tsunami, tsunami,
The first bit of water slipped me up,
I called for my friend, but by that time, it was too late.

**Michael Lewis  (9)**
**St Paul's Catholic Primary School, Portsmouth**


# Fireworks And Bonfire Night

Screaming rockets whizzing up in the sky
Children laughing with joy
With sparklers crackling in their hands
As they laugh, saying we love fireworks
Spinning Catherine wheels
Beautiful fireworks shooting up, up, up
Zooming rockets that explode in the air
The fireworks go sizzling, popping and banging
It sounds beautiful
I'm glad I was here tonight
Because it is Bonfire Night
This is the best day of my life.

**Shannon McKnight  (10)**
**St Paul's Catholic Primary School, Portsmouth**

# Tsunami

A big tsunami came to town
For everyone it was a frown
For they knew their houses would be washed away
That wouldn't be their day.

Lots of people are going to die
Instead of enjoying a lovely steak pie
This day has been very sad
With children losing mums and dads.

Hip, hip, hooray, no more tsunamis!
Now we can play every day
Now people can pay
For the food they need every day.

**Harry Haskett  (9)**
**St Paul's Catholic Primary School, Portsmouth**


# Whizzing, Fizzing

Up, up, up, they go
Flying in the cold winter's snow
The sky is filled with luminous reds, blues and greens
Holy moly, there's a Catherine wheel coming this way
It blows me into a pile of muddy hay
Bing, bang, pop, it flows up my top.

Fizz, fizz, up they whiz
Bursting into the open air
It hurtles into people's ears.

**Samuel Kind  (10)**
**St Paul's Catholic Primary School, Portsmouth**

# Tsunami

I was sunbathing on the beach,
When a person got up,
It was a little girl,
She started shouting,
I felt a chill run up my spine,
I looked up,
There was an enormous wave,
I was shocked . . .
But I still ran.

I looked back,
Millions of people were running up the beach,
Birds were flying,
Bodies were in the water,
My friend was one of them,
The wave was getting closer.

I ran down the street,
People were screaming,
Shouting and crying,
The wave was right behind me,
Rushing water,
I ran inside,
I closed my eyes,
I never opened them again.

**Cormac Dreelan  (9)**
**St Paul's Catholic Primary School, Portsmouth**


# My Feelings

I could hear the dogs barking.
I could see the clouds swaying.
I could feel the air dancing.
I could taste the yummy hot dogs.
I could smell the dirty smoke.

**Gail Sabadera  (7)**
**St Paul's Catholic Primary School, Portsmouth**

# Fireworks Light

Every year when fireworks light,
You always hear an echo in the night
And when you see the bonfire lit,
It warms you up a little bit,
All the kinds of fireworks you've never seen before,
You'll be surprised at what the people have in store.

All the colours, red and blue,
What is the best colour that suits you?

Do you like sparklers or big, booming ones,
Or do you like Catherine wheels, sparkling, spinning ones?
All the rest is Guy Fawkes, who tried to blow up Parliament,
He tried to do his best, but did not succeed!

**Imogen Rose  (9)**
**St Paul's Catholic Primary School, Portsmouth**


# Tsunami

I got up in the morning and my mum called out to me,
'Come and look at this, come onto the roof of the house.'
So I went on the roof and I couldn't believe my eyes.
I saw the most enormous wave that I had ever seen.

It was shocking to see, the street I was living on, so peaceful last week,
Now, to think that it's the most horrible street.
There were waves as big as a mountain, coming over us
Cars crashing into each other.

I was scared when I saw the enormous wave coming towards me,
I heard lots of people shouting and praying.
I was worried and all that we could do was sit and watch,
I hoped for some kind of miracle.

**Chloe Rye-Kerr  (9)**
**St Paul's Catholic Primary School, Portsmouth**

# Tsunami

Winds howling
people shouting
dead fish
wave crashing

Tsunami

Scared
astonished
ill and sick
tasted of
water

Tsunami

Crashing
shouting
screaming
praying

Tsunami.

**Nathan Cripps  (9)**
**St Paul's Catholic Primary School, Portsmouth**


# Tsunami

A light shines down
onto the people
who got struck by the tsunami
broken hearts
dead bodies
bodies in water
family dead
some lucky
sad families
who are as sad as me
it is very bad
we hope that it does not happen again.

**Holly Duckett  (9)**
**St Paul's Catholic Primary School, Portsmouth**

# Tsunami

I was looking at the beach
Suddenly, I was trembling with fear
I got my child and ran
My child was confused.

All I could see was a wall of water
Bodies floating and people running
I had to run to save my life.

The wave sounded like thunder
There was a big crash
A house has fallen down
And trapped my child.

Everything was silent
I was choking
The wave had hit me into a car
I thought I had broken my back
I could not open my eyes
That's when I knew I was dead.

**Brett Togwell (9)**
**St Paul's Catholic Primary School, Portsmouth**


# Tsunami

I could sense the waves coming towards me
I was scared
I hurried to tell people
To hurry up
But they did not listen
The waves were as big as a mountain
Everyone was starting to run
I saw people dying
I know I was going to get hit
I was looking for the tsunami
It hit my mum and dad.

**Ryan Morgan (9)**
**St Paul's Catholic Primary School, Portsmouth**

# Tsunami

I yelled at them,
They ignored me again,
But one small boy looked
And took off the fish he hooked.

He started to cry,
No one knew why,
But they began to understand
And fell down in the sand.

They ran away,
Not all live to this day,
Because of the tsunami.

**Siân Doherty (9)**
St Paul's Catholic Primary School, Portsmouth

# Tsunami

I saw it big and blue,
I was scared, just like you.

I had never seen one before,
So I watched, in awe.

I screamed and yelled,
The corpses smelled.

I didn't die,
But I did cry.

I hated that tsunami.

**Jacob Adolphe (9)**
St Paul's Catholic Primary School, Portsmouth

# Tsunami

It's coming near,
The tsunami,
You can hear the thunder,
Of the wave,
You can see it coming
And boats rowing towards shore,
People running away,
It's hit shore.

All you can hear,
Is smashing windows
And people praying to God.

You can hear the bikes scraping,
On the floor
And houses collapsing,
People are screaming,
I couldn't move.

But there it hit me,
If I went onto a mountain,
I would be safe,
I will bring some people with me
And I will be a hero.

**Sam Higgins  (9)**
**St Paul's Catholic Primary School, Portsmouth**


# Tsunami

First, I saw a big explosion,
Then, a lot of people running in fright.
Next, in Asia, for miles and miles
And when it was finished,
It was like the tsunami
And the sea as red as blood.

I bet they worried a lot
And so we are afraid all day.

**Conor Payne  (9)**
**St Paul's Catholic Primary School, Portsmouth**

## Winter Haiku

Winter, winter snow
Falling on my toes and nose
Bless you! Bless you! *Brrrrrrr!*

**Gabrielle Tierling (9)**
St Swithun Wells Catholic Primary School, Eastleigh


## Girls Haiku

Girls are very cool
Boys don't even rule the school
Girls have the power!

**Rebecca Platt (8)**
St Swithun Wells Catholic Primary School, Eastleigh


## Bugs Haiku

Spiders are creepy
Ants are all over the place
Cockroaches are worse!

**Rajan Rattan (9)**
St Swithun Wells Catholic Primary School, Eastleigh


## Animals Haiku

Animals are great
There are lots of creepy types
I don't like spiders!

**Josephine Brennan Bavington (9)**
St Swithun Wells Catholic Primary School, Eastleigh

# Homework Or PE Haiku

Football is the best
PE always gets a mess
Homework is the worst!

**Matthew Dolbear  (8)**
St Swithun Wells Catholic Primary School, Eastleigh

# About School Haiku

I love art and school
I like reading lots of books
I have lots of friends.

**Jacque Harris  (9)**
St Swithun Wells Catholic Primary School, Eastleigh

# Books Haiku

Books are good to read
I like doing art the best
I hate doing work.

**Craig Mellor  (9)**
St Swithun Wells Catholic Primary School, Eastleigh

# Summer Haiku

Summer is hot, hot
Summer is hot and warm, yes
That's the best of all!

**Danielle Coombs  (9)**
St Swithun Wells Catholic Primary School, Eastleigh

# Animals Haiku

I love animals
Peacocks have beautiful tails
Animals are cool!

**Shannon Lima  (8)**
**St Swithun Wells Catholic Primary School, Eastleigh**


# Romans Haiku

The Romans are cool
The Romans are excellent
The Romans are great!

**Tyron Prentice  (9)**
**St Swithun Wells Catholic Primary School, Eastleigh**


# Ode To A Bed

Oh, my wondrous bed
I adore you in every way.
I love your smoothness.
I am grateful for your softness and warmth.
I marvel at your height and the way you creak.
I love bouncing on your luxurious mattress.

**Kayleigh Thompson  (9)**
**Sharps Copse Primary School**


# Shadows

'I can make shadows,'
Dad said to me,
He made a rabbit, a cow and a tree.
'Now you make a shadow,'
Dad said to me,
So I made a monster.
Shadows don't scare me!

**Alexandra King  (7)**
**Sharps Copse Primary School**

# Ode To My Bed

Oh, my spectacular bed
I adore you in every way.
I admire jumping on your wonderful covers.
I cherish your silver poles and I like whacking.
I like scratching your stomach and tickling your back.
I like to sleep on your mattress.
I like sleeping on your beautiful mattress,
You make me scratch my face.
I like to hug you every day.
I like to throw stuff at you.

**Thomas Smith  (10)**
**Sharps Copse Primary School**


# The Stream

The slipping and swirling stream
Running down the hillside like a strike of lightning.
The tall and towering trees leaning over the edge
Like the shine off a whale's tail.
The rocky, reef river sauntering like a snail wandering in the snow.
The broken, battered bridge stretching like a snowy swan's wings
Spreading into the deep pond.

**Matthew Saunders  (10)**
**Sharps Copse Primary School**


# Ode To A Hamster

Oh, my wondrous hamster,
I adore you in every way.
Your silky fur is adorable and smooth.
Your white, sharp teeth nibble at hard carrots.
I worship your black, beady eyes and your black, button nose.
I cherish the way you come to me when I call you.
You inspire me to worship you.

**Kayleigh Roberts  (9)**
**Sharps Copse Primary School**

# Ode To My Fish

Oh fish,
Oh, wondrous fish
I admire the way you swim round the plants and under the bridge.
I like the way you play with plastic gems and crystals.
I worship you when my baby sister comes in and you hide.
You are the king of kings.
I'm grateful even though you don't know whether you are hungry or not.
But I like your gold body and white fins
And you swim like a bullet with your friend, Mike.
I adore you both.

**Shaun Eckstein  (9)**
**Sharps Copse Primary School**


# Ode To My Girlfriend

Oh, wondrous girl,
You charm me in every way.
I am glad to see your eyes,
They make an impression on me,
They make me really happy.
Your hair is sparkly, like the moon glinting at me.
The jokes that you say make me giggle.
You are the most wondrous girl,
The boys would always think of you.
When you kiss me on the cheek,
My heart beats like a speeding bullet.

**Tristan Jobber  (9)**
**Sharps Copse Primary School**

# Ode To My Bath

Oh, my wonderful bath.
You are so special in every way.
You clean me loads and loads.
You clean me soft and very, very smooth.
You inspire me with everything you do.
You are so thoughtful wherever you or I go.
You are helpful and kind.
You are so fresh, I praise your mint flavoured toothpaste stains.
I love to lie on you beneath the shining sunlight.
I love the racket you make when I slip in the water.

**Mollie Parker (9)**
**Sharps Copse Primary School**


# Ode To My Remote Control Car

Oh, my wondrous remote control car.
I get you really muddy, you still don't mind.
You are my shiny, zappy Zeus.
You are my excellent eagle,
My controller of the wind.
Your brakes are so good that you flip over.
You are my king.
You jump and slide.
I take you racing.
Sometimes you break, because cars smack your wheels.
You are my cheetah.

**Jordan Goodwin (9)**
**Sharps Copse Primary School**

# Ode To My Bike

Oh, my wondrous bike you are so brilliant.
I adore you in every way.
I admire the way you stand out to me.
I worship the thick, black tyres.
Oh bike, you are so beautiful and fast,
But slow up hills.
My splendid bike you are marvellous.
You, bike, are so adorable and you are the perfect bike for me.
Oh bike, your colour is purple and silver.
Oh bike, you are the best bike in the whole world.

**Alex MacDonald (9)**
**Sharps Copse Primary School**


# Ode To My Jewellery Box

Oh, my wondrous jewellery box,
I adore you in every way.
I love your amazing colours and your soft material.
I worship your different compartments
And that you are so small.
When I open you, you play a lovely tune.
I cherish your sound.
You make me feel happy when you play your tune.

**Sarah Clarke (9)**
**Sharps Copse Primary School**


# Ode To My Phone

Oh, my wondrous phone
You are so splendid and beautiful.
I adore you and you forgive me when I play on you.
You light up when I click one of your keys
And so do your buttons.
You have brilliant wallpaper
And a good background too.

**Ben Butt (9)**
**Sharps Copse Primary School**

# Ode To My Bed

Oh, my wondrous bed,
I adore your beautiful smell.
You bring a tiredness to my head.
Every time I smack you, you creak.
When I fall asleep, you keep me so warm.
I worship your silver bars.
I cherish your softness.
I love my inspiring pillow.
I appreciate the fact that you let my teddies lie on you.

**Ellie-Mae Matthews (9)**
**Sharps Copse Primary School**


# Ode To A Drum

Oh, my spectacular drum,
I adore you in every way.
I admire the crash and bash of your beats.
I cherish your silver shinyness.
I worship your long, blue, rusty edges.
You treat me with respect
Even though I hit you hard and roughly.
You inspire me to make you happy.

**Zac Watson (10)**
**Sharps Copse Primary School**


# Ode To My Girlfriend

Oh, my wondrous girlfriend,
I adore your blonde hair, it is clean and shiny.
Your beautiful smile makes me happy.
Your beautiful blue eyes are my favourite colour.
I adore your clean hands.
I adore it when you kiss me on the cheek,
My heart pumps like a speeding bullet.
You are cute and nice.

**Marley Palmer (9)**
**Sharps Copse Primary School**

## World War II

W hen the siren wailed
O ver the terrified land
R ed for death, flashes over England
L ight fades away
D eath awaits

W hatever you do
A nd wherever you go
R uining the war would be joy

II          everyone.

**Natasha Davis  (10)**
**Tanners Brook Junior School**


## Sad

Sad looks black and grey
Sad sounds like a fight
Sad is a terrible thing
We don't work, that is sad.

Sad is horrid, unhappy too
Sad is a terrible thing
You don't want to be sad forever
Don't be sad, be happy.

**Megan Cave  (9)**
**Tanners Brook Junior School**


## Fun

Fun is colours of the rainbow
Fun is playing with our friends
Fun is making new friends
Fun is going to the fair
Fun is when you care, care, care!

**Kirstin McKinven  (10)**
**Tanners Brook Junior School**

# The Fear Poem

Fear is the colours white, black and red.
It feels like you're in a room full of ghosts.
It feels like you've seen your worst nightmare.
Fear is when you're in a room and the door shuts,
Then you jump.
Fear is when you hear funny noises at night.
*Ooooh, aaahhh!*
Fear is when you get chased by mummies.
Fear is worse at Hallowe'en.
Fear is when you're walking
And bats fly over your head.
Fear is when you turn into a wolf,
Then you are walking
And you see a man with a knife.
You say, 'No!'
Then you're dead.

**Natasha Grogan  (10)**
**Tanners Brook Junior School**


# Air Raid

The siren sounds
Sending the message of death occurring.
Staring through windows
Into a gloomy darkness,
Only being able to witness
A sea of red and grey.

The taste of blood in my mouth,
Not being able to escape from it.
The pounding of my heart,
Like one thousand soldiers
Striding towards my destination,
Of being able to walk with pride.

**Robin Moran  (9)**
**Tanners Brook Junior School**

# Fear

Fear is like a bullet from a gun,
You want to run,
But no, you're rooted to the ground,
Until you are found.

Fear is like a lightning bolt,
Striking you from the sky,
It travels through your body,
You feel danger nearby.

Fear is dark, scary and exciting,
All at the same time,
You're all alone,
You hear a clock chime.

When midnight,
You hear the wind howl,
Upstairs,
Something is on the prowl.

Try and avoid fear,
If you can,
'Cause when that bullet strikes you,
you're helpless as a lamb.

**Dominic Ford  (10)**
**Tanners Brook Junior School**

# Ancient Egypt

I am Khufu and I can see pyramids,
Gods in the sky
And people doing all the work they should.
I see the city with new constructions,
Workers doing their jobs.
I see a workhouse,
Windmills with flour and rye bread
Coming out of the baker's house.

**James Tilley  (9)**
**Tanners Brook Junior School**

# Soldier

I am a soldier seeing dead bodies
I am a soldier, I am scared
I am a soldier, missing my family
I am a soldier, I am lonely.

I am a soldier hearing loud bangs
I am a soldier, I am scared
I am a soldier loading my gun
I am a soldier, I am lonely.

I am a soldier smelling the fear
I am a soldier, I am scared
I am a soldier running to fight
I am a soldier, I am lonely.

I am a soldier touching my gun
I am a soldier, I am scared
I am a soldier fighting the fight
I am a soldier, I am lonely.

I am a soldier tasting the victory
I am a soldier, I am scared
I am a soldier on my way home
I am a soldier, will I be lonely?

**Luke Harris & Jack Lazarski  (10)**
**Tanners Brook Junior School**


# World War II

When the siren went off, like a crazy rhino,
My family was scared and were hugging each other.
Ready or not, we all evacuated.
Lilly, my sister, died.
Dad was in the war as well.
World War II started now
And my family was terrified.
Rooney, my best cousin, was just about alive.

**Arjan Purewal  (9)**
**Tanners Brook Junior School**

# Tree

I am a small tree,
I can see children playing,
I can hear the birds tweeting
And the river flowing.
The wind is like a howling wolf.
I wish I had a friend,
But not humans, I'm scared of them.
I can feel the wind touch my leaves.
When it's night I can see cute animals.
I hear the owls hooting and I close my eyes.
I wake up and smell the sweet grass,
I smell the beautiful flowers,
They make me feel happy.
I love being a tree.

**Rebecca Grogan (10)**
**Tanners Brook Junior School**


# My Best Friends

Natasha's really nice,
She likes to eat rice,
Sometimes she is mad,
But hardly ever sad.
Rebecca's really fun,
She likes to eat iced buns,
She's really, really cute,
She never wears a suit.
These are my best friends,
Right until our ends.

**Greta Birch (9)**
**Tanners Brook Junior School**

# Feelings In War

She is terrified,
She is so devastated,
Now that she's lonely.

She is empty now,
Help me, I am anxious,
I know that he's gone.

I am hopeful now,
It is unbelievable,
I am so shattered.

**Elisha Hawkins  (10)**
**Tanners Brook Junior School**


# Feelings In War

She is petrified
Everything is shattered now
People feel destroyed.

She is destroyed now
Three sons are lonely and sad
People's hearts broken.

Thousands of men dead
All the time they lie in mud
What a waste of life.

**Jack Weatherington  (10)**
**Tanners Brook Junior School**


# Anger

Anger is like a black hole of fire.
Anger is like going on fire
And when you are angry, you go mad.

**Ali Hemy  (10)**
**Tanners Brook Junior School**

# Fish

I'm a little, little fish
In a great big pond.
I can see all my friends
Swimming happily along.
I can feel seaweed tickling my fin.
But most of all
I can hear dolphins
Splishing, splashing and sploshing
In the big, wide ocean.

**Abigail James (10)**
**Tanners Brook Junior School**


# Fear

Fear is *hot*
Fear is *light-headed*
Fear is like you are in a *box*
Fear is *black* and *red*
Fear is *sweaty*
Fear is *scary*
Fear is *frightening*
*Never feel afraid.*

**Harpreet Kaur Potiwal (9)**
**Tanners Brook Junior School**


# Untitled

I see people shooting,
I hear banging, killing and houses falling down,
I feel sad, lonely and scared,
I am running and hiding,
I see blood,
I am a soldier.

**Brandon Shephard (9)**
**Tanners Brook Junior School**

# Feelings In War

She is so shattered,
Everything is destroyed now,
Her husband died in the war.
I am so hungry, help me,
I am so anxious, now I am alone.
I am hopeful now.
It is unbelievable,
My children have gone.

**Harpage Kaur Bhakar (10)**
Tanners Brook Junior School


# Feelings In War

She is terrified,
She has not got a husband,
He was killed in the war.
Baby is crying,
She doesn't know what to do,
So she screams and shakes.
I am so shattered,
Bombs are dropping down on the ground,
Sound booming loudly.

**Demi-Lea Grinsell (10)**
Tanners Brook Junior School


# I'm A Colourful Flower

I'm a colourful flower blowing in the breeze,
I can see people coming up to me.
I'm a colourful flower blowing in the breeze,
I feel sad when people pick me.
I'm a colourful flower blowing in the breeze,
I can hear the crunching of my stem,
So I feel really sad and hope I'm a flower again.

**Kirstie Browning (9)**
Tanners Brook Junior School

# World War Two

W hen the siren sound went off
O ther people ran, I was confused
R unning to find a shelter
L ooking at other people run
D o I get in the last shelter or not?

W hat will I do?
A re the planes coming? I hope not
R unning to get to the last shelter.

T wo soldiers were outside
W ar was here, oh no!
O h no, the air raid has come!

**Sophie Spicer (9)**
**Tanners Brook Junior School**


# World War II

W hen the sirens sounded
O ut to find the shelter
R ound the world children got evacuated
L ondon was bombed
D eath, ahhhh.

W ar had taken over the world
A ll of the people were worried
R unning into the air raid shelter

II          Get everyone to safety.

**Amy Harmsworth (10)**
**Tanners Brook Junior School**

# World War Two

W hen the war started
O h, I was so worried and scared, but I was
R ushing
L ike a horrid beast going to the shelters
D ucking my head on the way.

W here were my parents
A nd family members?
R ushing like I was

T o the shelters maybe, but
W ould they be safe in this horrid disgrace?
O h, I hope they will.

**Kaylee White  (9)**
**Tanners Brook Junior School**


# World War II

W hen the siren went off, I was scared
O r I was cuddling my mummy
R eady to come back in my house
L ily, my sister, was dead, while
D addy was fighting in the war.

W orld War II started in 1939
A cross England, the war is real
R oses make us remember them

II                              real.

**Nathan Earley  (9)**
**Tanners Brook Junior School**

# The Great Barrier Reef

If I could go swimming in the Great Barrier Reef,
It looks so golden it would tempt a thief.
There are many beautiful things in Australasia,
But nothing more beautiful than the coast of Australia.

There are dolphins and sharks,
Jellyfish and crabs which all like to lark.
Clownfish and angelfish, lobsters and starfish in the wonderful seas,
It is much more fascinating than the birds in the trees.

In the deep, dark waters there live a few squid
And other creatures that are soon to be discovered.
How great it must be to find a new fish, undiscovered.
It's fun to be swimming and flapping
In the crystal clear waters of the Great Barrier Reef.

**Adam Kimber  (9)**
**Tanners Brook Junior School**


# Love

Love is like roses,
It's like you have been in the best of worlds.
It reminds you of when you've seen lots of daisies.
It's like a lovely taste of ice cream.
It feels like eating sweets.
It sounds like birds in the sky.

**Jessica Andrews  (8)**
**Tanners Brook Junior School**


# My Dad

My dad's a sleeping lion,
He lies in bed all day.
When he's really hungry,
He gets up to catch some prey.

**Elle Chivers  (10)**
**Tanners Brook Junior School**

# World War Two

W hen the siren started, I went
O ut and I made my way to the shelter.
R unning, running I was to the shelter.
L oud noises I could hear. I
D idn't come out, because I was scared.

W hen the noise went, I went outside to see if they had gone
A way. I had a look
R ound outside and they were still

T here, bombing houses and shooting people. I
W as scared, but there wasn't anything I could do.
O h, I hope I survive.

**Sophie Adams  (9)**
**Tanners Brook Junior School**


# Love

Love is peachy and smiley.
It sounds like kindness.
It tastes like a red rose.
It smells like a rose.
It looks like a ruby.
It feels like a heart falling from you.

**Jasvir Rathore  (9)**
**Tanners Brook Junior School**


# Fun

Fun is red, like a strawberry.
It reminds me of laughing.
It tastes of an orange.
It sounds like birds in a tree.
It smells like pizza.
It feels like a purring cat.

**Michael Harmsworth  (7)**
**Tanners Brook Junior School**

# Love

Love is red, like a scented rose.
Love reminds me of Valentine's Day.
Love sounds like the birds in the trees.
It tastes like a lovely strawberry.
It looks like a gleaming heart.
It smells like poppies in a field.
It feels like the gentle breeze.

**Ann-Marie Cummins (8)**
**Tanners Brook Junior School**


# Anger

Anger is black, like night-time.
It sounds like paper scrunching.
It tastes like burgers.
It smells like leaves.
It looks like Brussels sprouts.
It feels like people.

**Max Richings (8)**
**Tanners Brook Junior School**


# Love

Love is pink, like a love heart.
It sounds like a love song.
It tastes like a bowl of strawberries.
It smells like a garden of roses.
It looks like a happy couple.
It feels like kisses up your arms.

**Liberty Reeves (8)**
**Tanners Brook Junior School**

# Sadness

Sadness is blue, like the sky.
It sounds like ghosts.
It tastes like mud.
It smells like Pot Noodles.
It looks like a man.
It feels like a soft toy.
Love is happy, like red.
Anger is black, like the dark.

**Jack Sayers  (7)**
**Tanners Brook Junior School**


# Love

Love is red, like a beautiful rose.
It sounds like butterflies fluttering.
It feels like a smooth breeze.
It smells like a lovely daffodil.
It tastes like sweet cherries.
It reminds me of blossom off the tree.

**Terri-Ann Ryder  (8)**
**Tanners Brook Junior School**


# Laughter

Laughter is blue, like the sea.
It tastes like sweets.
It looks like children's smiles.
It feels like cotton.
It smells like daisies.
It sounds like the flute.

**Anna Godsell  (8)**
**Tanners Brook Junior School**

# Air Raid

The siren sounds,
My heart pounds.
It makes me feel unsafe.
The people run,
It's not fun,
I won't take the risk.
The all-clear sounds,
My heart slows down,
I now feel a bit safe.
People cease to run,
Time to have fun,
I am free from risks.

**Daisy Breed  (9)**
**Tanners Brook Junior School**


# Emotions In War

The bombs are falling
I feel really sad and scared
I see bombs in dreams
The bombs are falling
The noise crashing around me
The shelter is dark
The bombs are falling
The smell of fear fills the air
Hoping I survive.

**Steve Mundy  (10)**
**Tanners Brook Junior School**


# Fear

Fear is black, like a hole with a black, scary robot.
Fear sounds like howling noises.
Fear tastes like spiders.
Fear smells like prawns.

**Brooke Tomkins  (7)**
**Tanners Brook Junior School**

# Feelings In War

She felt terrified,
Hitler wants to rule the world,
Her five sons are dead,
Soldiers are dying,
Poppies growing everywhere,
People are destroyed.
Why do we need war?
What is it for today?
We must stand and fight.

**Gemma Short  (9)**
**Tanners Brook Junior School**


# Emotions In War

She is so destroyed,
The telegram has arrived,
Husband lost at sea.
Anxious, scared inside,
Shattered, destroyed, desolate.
Husband lost at sea.
Children home from school,
How will she tell the news?
Husband lost at sea.

**Kieran Joseph  (10)**
**Tanners Brook Junior School**


# Fear

Fear is as black as a light being switched off.
Fear is someone crying in a dark room.
Fear smells like burnt food.
Fear is something rotten.

**Josh Attwood  (8)**
**Tanners Brook Junior School**

# Feelings Of War

Her sons are dead,
All her sons' toys are gone,
The house is *destroyed.*

People have been killed,
Lives destroyed, homes in ruins
And what is it for?

Because of Hitler,
A man with a small moustache,
Her three sons are dead!

**Edward Sivyour  (10)**
**Tanners Brook Junior School**


# Feelings In War

She is so, so shattered,
Soldiers are petrified,
Everyone is sad,
Men are terrified,
Everyone is so lonely,
Kids are really sad,
Women are worried,
Men are unbelieving,
Kids are so lonely.

**Rhea Waters  (10)**
**Tanners Brook Junior School**


# Love

Love is red, like a beautiful rose
It reminds me of romantic love
It sounds like birds in the trees
It tastes like a lovely strawberry
It looks like a peaceful night
It smells like blossom on trees.

**Lucy Smith  (7)**
**Tanners Brook Junior School**

# Feelings In War

She has been destroyed
She has lost everyone
Son killed in the war.

Soldiers are scared
Soldiers are really hungry
She's shaking with fright
Desperate letters
Find out about her husband
She's been destroyed.

**Liam Gale  (9)**
**Tanners Brook Junior School**


# Hunger

Hunger is brown, like pizza.
It smells like good food.
It looks like chocolate.
It tastes like burgers.
It sounds like rumbling in my tummy.
It feels like magic.
It reminds me of a feast.

**Jack Evans  (8)**
**Tanners Brook Junior School**


# Silence

Silence is yellow, like a lemon
It reminds me of quietness
It feels like happiness
It looks like peace
It sounds like God
It tastes like juice
It smells like oranges.

**Connor Kenway  (7)**
**Tanners Brook Junior School**

# Love

Love is red.
It reminds me of a peaceful night.
It tastes like a ripe apple.
It smells like a red, red rose, as lovely as I've ever smelt.
It sounds like a harp playing.
It reminds me of a romantic dinner.
It feels like an arrow straight through your heart.

**Munraj Purewal  (8)**
**Tanners Brook Junior School**


# Love

Love is red, like a blooming rose
It tastes like chocolate
It smells like strawberries
It sounds like a piano sweetly playing
It reminds me of Valentine's Day
It feels like a romantic dinner
It looks like a gleaming star.

**Le'ana Montana  (7)**
**Tanners Brook Junior School**


# Hate

Hate is dark purple, like a bowling ball.
It sounds like nails screeching on a blackboard.
It tastes like mouldy cheese.
It smells like dry apricots.
It looks like tears dropping from a cloud.
It feels like jelly.

**Veronica Tebano  (7)**
**Tanners Brook Junior School**

# Frustration

Frustration is black, like the darkest hole.
It feels like the spiciest touches.
It smells like your mum cooking slugs.
It sounds like the chitter-chatter of bugs.
It tastes like paper.
It looks like an elf in the corner of your eye.
It reminds me of homework.

**Jack Gallacher  (8)**
**Tanners Brook Junior School**


# Silence

Silence is white, like a cloud.
It sounds like wind blowing softly.
It tastes like air.
It looks like a friendly ghost.
It feels like silky petals.
It reminds me of poetry.
It smells like flowers.

**Megan Ashford-Hett  (7)**
**Tanners Brook Junior School**


# Love

Love is red, like a rose.
It sounds like birds.
It tastes like cheese.
It smells like roses.
It looks like roses on the tree.
It feels like a ball.

**James Johnson  (7)**
**Tanners Brook Junior School**

## Emotions In War (Haikus)

She lost her husband
Now she is devastated
That war is over.

He is just destroyed
His house bombed and all is lost
Now he's lost his wife.

The boy is anxious
Worrying about his mum
She lost her husband.

**Mitchell Parker  (10)**
**Tanners Brook Junior School**

# Love

Love is red, like a rose tree.
It sounds like a beautiful bird.
It tastes like your first kiss.
It smells like romance.
It looks like a heart.
It feels like a good day.

**Jessica Eves  (7)**
**Tanners Brook Junior School**

# Love

Love is like a beautiful red rose.
It feels like pink blossom on the trees.
It smells like yellow daffodils.
It looks like a big, red heart.
The colour is a big arrow going through a heart.
It tastes like lots of sweets.

**Taylar Iason  (7)**
**Tanners Brook Junior School**

# Emotions In War

When will the boat land?
I am very scared right now,
Please come and save me.

I will get killed now.
Help me, I am terrified!
I am so hungry.

Unbelievable.
I can't even think right now,
I am so afraid.

**Harry Smith  (9)**
**Tanners Brook Junior School**


# Feelings In War

I am so lonely.
I miss my husband so much.
I want him back now.
It is horrible.
The baby won't stop crying.
What shall I do now?
This is tiring me.
This problem will not go away.
I am so lonely.

**Nicole Roberts  (9)**
**Tanners Brook Junior School**


# Happiness

Happiness is yellow, like a yellow butterfly.
It tastes like lovely bananas in a tree.
It reminds me of daffodils growing in a field.
It feels like eating sweets.
It sounds like laughing.

**Ashleigh Horeman  (7)**
**Tanners Brook Junior School**

# Feelings In War

It is so lonely
She is so devastated
Why did I do it?

She is so shattered
Help me, I am so anxious
I am terrified.

I am so hungry
Why did I let it happen?
I am so sad now.

**Ellis White  (10)**
**Tanners Brook Junior School**


# Anger

Anger is red, like a red volcano
It sounds like an exploding volcano
It tastes like a big ball in your brain
It smells like a burning candle
It looks like a big candle
It feels like I am going to explode.

**Jordan Hayball  (8)**
**Tanners Brook Junior School**


# Hate

Hate is green, like smelly pickles.
It sounds like a big drum banging in my head.
It tastes like a bitter onion.
It smells like a smelly sock.
It looks like a long sausage.
It feels like a pot of stinky water.

**Sean Neary  (7)**
**Tanners Brook Junior School**

# Love

Love is red, like a bleeding heart
It sounds like a thousand pieces of a heart
It tastes like a big kiss
It smells like red lipstick
It looks like bright red lips
It feels like a romantic day at the beach.

**Kerry Cook (7)**
**Tanners Brook Junior School**


# Anger

Anger is black and red
Anger seems like a lion catching its prey
Anger smells like hot chilli peppers in my head
Anger sounds like thunder
Anger is popular.

**Bethany Holman (9)**
**Tanners Brook Junior School**


# Love

Love is a deep red, like a massive ball of fluff
It sounds like someone's heart beating really fast
Love tastes like a big ball of sweet, flowery perfume
It looks like a huge red heart
It feels like a really soft heart.

**Chelsea Kenway (8)**
**Tanners Brook Junior School**


# Anger

Anger is red, like a volcano exploding
That comes out of nowhere.
It feels like a stone in my brain.

**Michael Bolton (7)**
**Tanners Brook Junior School**

# Sadness

Sadness is blue, like friends breaking up
It sounds like teardrops dropping from your eye
It tastes like bat blood
It smells like a volcano
It looks like a massive hole in your heart
It feels like heavy rain.

**Chelsey-Lea Mouland  (7)**
**Tanners Brook Junior School**


# Happiness

Happiness is orange and juicy, like fun.
It sounds like people giggling loudly.
It tastes like yummy strawberries.
It smells like smelly grapes.
It looks like a happy, cheery, smiley face.
It feels like I'm magically strong.

**Victoria Lambert  (7)**
**Tanners Brook Junior School**


# Love

Love is red, like bright roses.
It sounds like tweeting birds in my ear.
It tastes like yummy chocolate.
It smells like lovely perfume.
It looks like sweet lips.
It feels like a lovely day of happiness.

**Laura Challis  (7)**
**Tanners Brook Junior School**

# Fear

Fear is a tangy orange, like a black spider.
It sounds like a slimy snake hissing.
It tastes like evil vampire's blood.
It smells like chewy sweets.
It looks like crazy bats.
It feels like sticky slime.

**Molly Cole (8)**
**Tanners Brook Junior School**

# Laughter

Laughter is yellow, like a juicy lemon.
Laughter sounds like hyenas laughing.
Laughter tastes like yellow bananas.
Laughter smells like chewy sweets.
Laughter looks like happiness.
Laughter feels like being tickled.

**Michael Hudson (8)**
**Tanners Brook Junior School**

# Laughter

Laughter is yellow, like a sour lemon.
Laughter sounds like hyenas laughing.
Laughter tastes like curly bananas.
Laughter smells like sour sweets.
Laughter looks like happiness.
Laughter feels like a big, massive tickle.

**Bradley Bennett (8)**
**Tanners Brook Junior School**

## Anger

Anger is like a big volcano.
It sounds like a big noise.
It tastes like a red-hot pepper.
It smells like hot fire.
It looks like a big, pointy stone.
It feels like a bumpy stone.

**Tahnina Longman (8)**
**Tanners Brook Junior School**

## Happiness

Happiness is bright yellow, like laughing love.
It sounds like loud music.
It tastes like melting chocolate.
It smells like sweet roses.
It looks like children playing.
It feels like I'm floating on a fluffy cloud.

**Ellen Belcher (7)**
**Tanners Brook Junior School**

## Anger

Anger is red, like skull-burning fire.
It sounds like an ear-piercing scream.
It tastes like a ginormous puff of smoke.
It smells like a burning, smelly fag.
It looks like a ball of blazing fire.
It feels like a burning fire in my brain.

**Charlie Maddocks (7)**
**Tanners Brook Junior School**

# Fun

Fun is a lovely, bright, shiny yellow, like a big balloon
Like a huge, smiley sun
Like lots of happy people playing
Like lots of yummy fruits
Like lots of sugary sweets
Like the greatest faces in the world
Like playing lots.

**Courtney Skading  (7)**
**Tanners Brook Junior School**


# Love

Love is pink, like a beautiful rose.
It sounds like birds singing sweetly.
It tastes like melted chocolate inside your tummy.
It smells like a bunch of sweet flowers.
It looks like red hearts, floating around you.
It feels like a soft apple in your hands.

**Tia Wassell  (8)**
**Tanners Brook Junior School**


# Love

Love is red, like a heart.
It sounds like love in my heart.
It tastes like a bar of chocolate.
It smells like a lovely sweet.
It looks like a boy and girl.
It feels lovely and smooth.

**Sarah Toye  (7)**
**Tanners Brook Junior School**

# Auschwitz

I am starved,
I am gone.
I hope I will be saved
Because the light has shone.

I will die,
I will pay.
I hope they won't
Say what they say.

I have been told
To kill my friends,
I don't want to, but if I don't
It will be the end.

I am in a chamber now,
Strapped to my seat.
The gas is on –
All I can do is weep.

**Tim Robinson  (10)**
**The Crescent Primary School**


# Why?

All the people see is death,
Soon they'll be nothing but flesh.

They point guns at the children,
They get satisfaction when they kill them.

Is it fair to kill the Jew?
They are human beings too.

The Jews are burned until they die,
The Germans laugh and watch them fry.
So please, tell me why.

**Louise Matthews  (10)**
**The Crescent Primary School**

## Auschwitz Birkenau

We were forced into chambers,
Surrounded with barbed wire.
We were stripped of clothing,
Watching dead bodies burn in fire.
Every now and then,
The moan of someone dying,
Every now and then,
The whimper of a child crying.
Someone being shot,
Falls to the ground and dies.
This is a terrible place,
No doubt about it.
I think I'll go and join the people
Saying their last goodbyes.

**Maddie Smith  (10)**
**The Crescent Primary School**

## Auschwitz

Suffering lies in a soldier's mind,
As he takes a dagger to a Jew's chest,
One million bodies are burnt to a crisp,
As the Nazis laugh with an evil hiss.
People are praying for help,
But all they can do is live in misery,
Innocent Jews are now being hunted,
Now the soldiers have what they wanted.
All we can do now is look back in history,
At the suffering years of World War II.

**Chloe Ashford  (10)**
**The Crescent Primary School**

# The Gates Of Auschwitz

The gates of Auschwitz open,
As my heart is slowly broken,
We Jews have no will,
Against the Nazis' thirst to kill.
We are stripped of our clothes,
Our fate will soon be chose,
Dead bodies are piled naked and bare,
Soon to be no more, by fire's red flare.
A mother rocks her child, who is no more,
For she has suffered the death of this war,
We will soon be gassed and shot,
And what for? And for what?

The gates of Auschwitz open,
My heart is already broken.

**Hannah McGeachy  (11)**
**The Crescent Primary School**

# Suffering

The snipers in their hands,
The hunger they go through,
The times that they are trapped,
Their freedom is now gone.

The tears in their eyes,
The braveness that they hold,
The traces of the body,
The agonies they're in.

The sadness on their faces,
The horror of the death,
The bones of their bodies,
Why can't they be let free?

**Daniel Whitlocke  (11)**
**The Crescent Primary School**

# Sadness

Sadness, destruction, pain,
And all this for a little grain.
People's lives destroyed in an instant,
They should be free, others say they shouldn't.
Belief doesn't matter,
Why should their hearts shatter?
Nazis should be the ones who suffer,
Locked away so no one can see them.
*But*, it's too late, it's done now,
So I hope you trip, when you take your bow.

**Paige Dietman-Hesketh  (11)**
**The Crescent Primary School**


# Holocaust

How could humans do that?
They are just like us, so why do that?
Cooped up in gas chambers,
Or made to shoot their neighbours,
Stripped, beaten, starved,
No more gentle laughing,
They're dead.

**Katie Smith  (10)**
**The Crescent Primary School**


# My Cat, Daisy

My cat has a habit of gobbling her food,
Then going to sleep.
She goes to the toilet in my dad's herb garden
And she always gets a wallop for that.
My cat is the most colourful cat in the world.
She is brown, black, white and a ginger colour.
About six o'clock in the morning she mews, *mews!*

**Zachary Baxter-Hill  (7)**
**The Grey House School**

# Spots

I hop from lily pad to lily pad,
M y webbed feet stick to each lily pad,

A s I am about to jump, I

F all into the water. My
R ed spots show from above.
O ver and under, avoiding the hungry
G reen frogs as I turn. As

W inter comes, so
I ce comes too.
T ime to go and find another
H ome and start again.

R ed spots can't be seen from above,
E ven when I move away from the
D ark, cold mud that

S urrounds me. After the cold months, I return to the
P ond.
O ver and under I go, avoiding
T he other hungry frogs with
S pots.

**Lily Stevens  (11)**
**The Grey House School**


# My Dad

My dad plays rugby with a ball,
It hardly has a pattern at all.
I think you'll find he rather likes it,
Even though I've never tried it.

My dad's a very bad dad,
He never has a moment free.
Once, he went to play rugby,
Without giving me my tea!

**Jasmine Hellings  (8)**
**The Grey House School**

# Teachers' Homes

Their homes would be plain, boring, bold
And our music teacher
Would have a big piano and music on the floor.

Our science teacher would have a photo of a volcano
And a room for tests.
She takes plants and goes out in the garden,
She has a big cooking pot and sometimes she takes children,
But no one knows what she does with them.

Our maths teacher would have
A white board and pictures and radio.
Our French teacher would have pictures of France
And a big room with French things.

Our computer teacher is normally normal,
But I think he's got a secret that I'm not supposed to know.
He's sometimes on the phone, but he never says who he's talking to
So I think he's a mystery man.

**Chloe Young  (11)**
**The Grey House School**


# Springtime

By the feel of the warmth of the golden sun,
It makes me know that spring has begun.
Crocus fill your garden lawn,
Opening up at the crack of dawn.

The primrose scent is sweet and good,
You can find it in springtime in any wood.
Thousands of bluebells on the ground,
Out of the grass and all around.

There are daffodils, tulips and daisies too,
It makes the garden seem brand new.
I love this time of year best of all,
When it takes longer and longer for night to fall.

**Tara Kirby  (9)**
**The Grey House School**

# The Lion

He was standing proudly in the hot summer sun,
But not for no reason.
He was looking for food, but hadn't found anything.
His brown ears twitched, trying to track sound.
And then . . .
He heard . . .
A sound . . .
Coming towards him.
He turned around and there,
In front of him, was a herd of deer.
He spotted an adult deer and went for it,
As fast as he could.
He got it and killed it
With one quick bite of its neck.
He took the carcass back to his pride
And they all ate that evening.

**Samantha Fuhrmann  (10)**
**The Grey House School**


# Tsunami Disaster

In many countries, people you see dying,
Loved ones are lost, people are crying.
We must help them, we must try,
How would you like it if your family were to die?

Many of these countries were quite poor,
Now they are, more.
These people have no homes
And we waste money on mobile phones.

What have affected people ever done
To lose a family member, maybe a son?
All this happened the day after Christmas,
In the month of December 2004.

**Taliesin Manasvi Tyagi  (10)**
**The Grey House School**

# All Grown Up

When I'm grown up I want to be
An artist!
And travel all around the world to sell my paintings.

When I'm grown up I want to be
A fashion model!
And be in newspapers and magazines
And walk on the red carpet in combats.

When I'm grown up I want to be
A famous horse rider!
And win lot of championships
With lots of medals and trophies.

*When I'm grown up I want to do*
*All these things,*
*But at the same time, live in*
*The same house I live in now!*

**Mariella Hancock (10)**
**The Grey House School**


# Freddy

Freddy is a puppy with a red collar.
He is my favourite dog.
He always talks to me and tells me his secrets.
He loves to play football!
He watches TV in my room, until he's tired.
Freddy's so clever 'cause he can read and tell the time.
His friend is Scruffy.
He supports Arsenal FC.
He is naughty and fat.

**Samuel Hopson (7)**
**The Grey House School**

# School's Out!

Sitting in the classroom bored to death
Then goes the bell, thank goodness for that.

It's spring break, spring break
Spring break, spring break! School's out! Yippee!

We're going to France, I can't wait for that
But first it's homework, how boring is that?

It's spring break, spring break
Spring break, spring break! School's out! Yippee!

We're staying in a villa, it's got its own pool
And I won't even be thinking of school!

It's spring break, spring break
Spring break, spring break! School's out! Yippee!

We're going go-kart racing, how cool is that?
I'm not thinking of maths or my SATs.

It's spring break, spring break
Spring break, spring break! School's out! Yippee!

**Cameron Gaul**
**The Grey House School**


# Tsunami, Tsunami

Tsunami! First a quake,
Get to high ground, for goodness sake.

Look out, a tidal wave's coming,
Come on, we'd better start running.

People dropping to the floor,
There's gonna be an awful lot more.

Hundreds of thousands of lives are lost,
As the waves tumbled and tossed.

It was over oh, so fast,
But in our memory it will last.

**Jordan Brannan (10)**
**The Grey House School**

# Tsunami Wave!

A normal day,
Nothing much to say,
Suddenly I saw it,
A great towering wall of water.

Now everyone is looking at the wave,
But then the water came tumbling down,
I was horrified, amazed.
People running to high ground,
People climbing up trees for safety,
I heard screaming,
I saw my best friend's house being chewed and swallowed up
                                                          by the wave.

The wave was coming deeper, deeper into the village,
Then the wave died back.
People had so many losses,
People in despair,
Will take years to repair.
A devastating sight,
Is the 26th of December.

**Alex Hayes  (9)**
**The Grey House School**


# Tsunami!

Veterans of the tsunami, lives are filled with terror,
Burned in their minds forever and ever.
Losing a friend, a son or a daughter,
Lungs filled up with litres of water.
Two hundred islands in the Maldives,
Take away six that were lost forever.
Sixty seconds of absolute terror,
Not to be forgotten forever and ever.
The earth has been scarred
On 26th of December.

**Blair Morrison  (9)**
**The Grey House School**

# The Seasons

Spring is full of colour,
Summer is very hot,
Autumn is one massive leaf,
Winter is cold and crispy.

Spring has flowers and life,
Summer has wasps and sun,
Autumn has leaves and rain,
Winter has snow and ice.

Spring is full of blossom trees,
Summer is full of sunshine,
Autumn is full of raking up leaves,
Winter is full of joy and laughter.

Spring brings new life,
Summer brings little bumblebees,
Autumn brings shades of brown, red, yellow and orange,
Winter brings snowflakes, all different shapes.

Spring brings colour to the world,
Summer brings playtime and sunbathing,
Autumn brings falling leaves, floating off trees,
Winter brings Christmas and a new year for us all.

**Alexandra Moore  (10)**
**The Grey House School**


# Wave Of Cruelty

Sri Lanka was a normal place,
Now the smile is wiped off everyone's face.
It's said to measure 8.9,
This cause is truly not divine.
450 miles of cracks were found,
Under the seabed in the ground.
We are lucky, you and me,
We're not floating out to sea.
Some just on holiday enjoying life,
The tidal wave was like a plunging knife.

**Katharine Whittingham  (9)**
**The Grey House School**

# With Love From Anne

I was lying on the beach,
Sitting all alone,
Suddenly I heard screaming,
I looked at the sea.
An enormous wave!
Metres and metres high!
I ran to Mother, to find cover,
We climbed up a tree,
Oh! Please don't be!
The calm sea erupted,
The blue sky turned to grey.
The silence filled with screams.
I squeezed my eyes shut
And held my mother's hand tight.
We waited for at least an hour,
Then suddenly it stopped.
I opened my eyes, *nothing!*
People crying! People sighing!
Trees knocked down.
But oh,
Survivors!

    With love from Anne.

**Louise Ingham  (10)**
**The Grey House School**


# My Cat

My cat is all ginger,
He's fat and furry too.
He is quite annoying.
I know he's going to die soon,
But I will always love him, whatever he does.
He is ginger, like gingerbread
And he is like a big, fat toy.

**Adam Byles  (7)**
**The Grey House School**

# Autumn Puzzle

Swirling, whirling,
Down I go,
In the wood,
From the trees,
What am I?

Silent I go,
Down, down.

Twirling, whirling,
Red as the fire,
Yellow as lemon,
Brown as timber,
What am I?

Silent I go,
Down, down.

Twirling, whirling,
On the forest floor
I fall,
As silent as the golden eagle's swoop.

Silent I go,
Down, down.

I am your dream,
I am your wonder,
I am the leaves,
Of the world in wonder.

**Charlotte Fowles  (10)**
**The Grey House School**

# Pets

I wish I had a horse
The shed would be a stable
I'd ride it every day of course
If only I was able

I wish I had a dolphin
And a garden pool
As we swim, I hold his fin
That would be so cool

I wish I had a donkey
His name it would be Bubble
If his legs were wonky
I would love him double.

**Lucie Lawton  (10)**
**The Grey House School**


# Rabbit

I have a rabbit called Fudgy,
She's colourful and pretty as a budgie.
She runs and jumps in the garden
And always says excuse my pardon.
She eats lots and lots of carrots
To keep away the parrots.
Her little tail is white,
She chewed our Christmas lights.
She chewed through the telephone wire,
She makes our lives quite dire.

**Yasmine Causer  (9)**
**Whiteley Primary School**

# There's A Monster In My Closet

There's a monster in my closet, I know it.
*Crash!* What was that? I know it.
*Screech!* Is it fat, I wonder?
*Bang!* Are there three, I wonder?
*Whoosh!* Or is it a tree, I wonder?

Last night it got really bad,
It drove me very mad.

*Crash!* Who was that? I know it.
*Screech!* Is it a cat? Can't be.
*Bang!* Is it a trick? Can't be.
*Whoosh!* By my mate Nick? Can't be.

Last night it got much worse,
It made me double curse.

*Crash!* Where was that? I know it.
*Screech!* Is it a bat? Might be.
*Bang!* Is it small? Might be.
*Whoosh!* Or is it tall? Might be.

It's giving my head a blister,
*'Boo!'*
Aarrgghh! It's my sister!

**George Upton  (10)**
**Whiteley Primary School**


# Horses

The horse was galloping on a sunny day,
Along came a girl with lots of hay.
A dog came running to follow her that way
And she said, 'But if you bark, you'll frighten the horses away.'
As the afternoon passed, she galloped away,
Through the woodlands and not the hay.
It was a beautiful day for the horses to ask,
'Can we do this more often?'

**Shannon Mitchell  (9)**
**Whiteley Primary School**

# Pants!

Pants are yellow, pants are blue,
Pants taste nice with turnip stew.
Pants are green, pants are red,
I've got a mouldy pair under the bed.
Pants of silver, pants of gold,
Some are new and some are old.
Pants have stripes, pants have spots,
Sometimes they're made out of old robots.
Pants worn high, pants worn low,
Even Robin Hood with his shiny bow.
Pants are wide, pants are thin,
When they are snapped, what a terrible thing.
Pants are flat, pants are frilly,
But they're only hard in Piccadilly.
Pants of violet, pants of green,
You only have them silk when you're a queen.
Pants of twenty, pants of two,
My mate was sick in them on loop the loop.
Pants of flowers, pants of cammo,
My great granddad lost 'em with his ammo.
Pants of steel, pants of wood,
I get gold ones when I'm good.
Pants are rich, pants are poor,
I found a pair outside my door.
Pants don't shout, pants don't wail,
I found a pair in the nest of a quail.
Pants are used, pants are worn,
My mate had his badly torn.
I love pants!

**James Wright  (10)**
**Whiteley Primary School**

# Fantasy Fun

Zoom, zoom, zoom
On a big baboon.
Fly, fly, fly
On a giant apple pie.
Run, run, run
On two cherry buns.
Climb, climb, climb
We're running out of time.
Spin, spin, spin
On a massive bin.
Whizz, whizz, whizz
Like a bottle full of fizz.
Jiggle, jiggle, jiggle
And make yourself giggle.
Dash, dash, dash
With a big, black moustache.
Buzz, buzz, buzz
In a bucket full of fuzz.
Float, float, float
On a long, pink boat.
Slip, slip, slip
On a banana strip.
Whirl, whirl, whirl
Like the pattern on a pearl.
Stomp, stomp, stomp
Like your mum in a grump.
Laugh, laugh, laugh
In a big bubble bath.
Play, play, play
On this fun fantasy day.

**Liam Frow  (9)**
**Whiteley Primary School**

# Snowflakes

Softly on the wind I blow
Dancing down to meet the snow
Meeting icicles as I go
Dancing down to meet the snow

I see squirrels finding nuts
Under my cold winter blanket
Dancing down to meet the snow

Finally I meet the snow
My journey has ended
On the white snow
It really is splendid.

**Georgia Sugden (8)**
**Whitewater CE Primary School**

# Autumn

The world has come to autumn and now the conkers are here.
The leaves are falling off the trees one by one,
Swirling, jiggling overhead.
Wind, wind blowing everywhere,
Conkers in pockets,
Falling down waiting to be found,
I do like autumn.

**Zoë Brooks (8)**
**Whitewater CE Primary School**

# Autumn

Autumn is here now,
The shiny, brown conkers slipping out
Of their bright green, prickly cases,
Scattering all over the thick beds of crispy, crunchy leaves,
Yellow, green, orange and gold.

**Isabella Galardo (8)**
**Whitewater CE Primary School**

# Autumn

Silver, sparkling mornings
Crisp and frosty air
Dancing, prancing, gliding leaves
Swooping and sliding in the north wind.
Flocks of birds flying south
Squawking and quacking overhead.
Lots of rainstorms, thunder and lightning
Crackle, crackle
These are the sounds of autumn.

**Christopher Cooper (8)**
**Whitewater CE Primary School**


# Autumn

Autumn is lots of different colours
That fall from the trees, flashing, swirling,
Twirling down.
Berries that fall from the trees to the ground,
To the children gathered below.
Hazelnuts falling as the squirrels
Catch them.

**Holly Barrett (8)**
**Whitewater CE Primary School**


# Autumn

Conker cases, green and prickly like a hedgehog's back,
Caramel brown, orangey yellow, dancing, prancing, swirling,
Beneath the trees, like a flaming fire.
Squirrels scurrying to collect their nuts to store up high,
Swooping, swaying like a glider, gliding down to the ground.
Hazelnuts falling for squirrels to collect.
I love autumn.

**Nerys Nabbs (8)**
**Whitewater CE Primary School**

# Autumn

Colourful, waving leaves
Trees' branches swaying in the wind
Conkers in their green, spiky shells
Crispy leaves scattered all over the ground
Animals getting ready to hibernate
I love autumn.

**Emma Morris  (8)**
**Whitewater CE Primary School**

# Autumn

Autumn is a lovely time to watch
The smoke twirling in the sky
And to watch the shiny, brown conkers
Peeping out of their green, spiky homes.

**Tristan Bushnell  (7)**
**Whitewater CE Primary School**

# Autumn

I love autumn,
Because I like collecting
Golden leaves
And I love shiny, brown conkers.

**Nicole Turner  (7)**
**Whitewater CE Primary School**

# Autumn

Autumn is leaves
Soon misty mornings and fresh chilly air.
See nuts falling all over the ground
See the good soil carefully ploughed.

**Megan Head  (8)**
**Whitewater CE Primary School**

# Christmas

He swiftly glides along the ground,
Floating on a mist that covers his knees.
His hair is like a blazing red winter's fire,
His eyes glisten like frozen crystals in the sun.

Many have seen glimpses of his shining face,
But nothing more.
What he is, you can't make out,
Where he lives you don't know,
All you know is that his name is Christmas.

**Imran Mair (11)**
**Whitewater CE Primary School**


# Autumn

Autumn time has come again,
Leaves twirling and swaying in the breeze,
Conkers scattered all over the ground,
Acorns twirling round and round,
Children playing in the leaves,
Squirrels in trees and on the ground,
Storing up for winter - and it is here!

**Freya Cooksley (8)**
**Whitewater CE Primary School**


# Winter

Softly silent, swirling snowflakes,
Sharp, glassy icicles pointing to the ground,
People ice skating on the frozen lakes,
Crunchy snow all around,
Snowflakes falling to the ground,
Snow is children's favourite thing.

**Jade Capon (7)**
**Whitewater CE Primary School**

# Autumn

Autumn's like a brown world,
Leaves spinning, gliding as they fall.
Whirling, wonderful sparks of fire
Falling to the ground.
Green, spiky conker shells
Covered by fiery leaves.
Hazelnuts diving to the ground, disappearing
As they get picked up by brown squirrels.
Autumn's here at last!

**Bethany O'Sullivan (8)**
**Whitewater CE Primary School**


# Autumn

Autumn is the time for playing in the leaves,
Autumn is the time for people with their rakes.
Conkers on the road looking like hedgehogs, scattered everywhere,
Flames in the sky from bonfires on the ground.
Fireworks in the sky, exploding up high, looking at the ground,
Are conkers to be found?
All around are acorns on the ground to be found.
Winter is here now.

**Bob Johnson (8)**
**Whitewater CE Primary School**


# Autumn

From the highest branches to the lowest burrows
Grows the autumn mist on the sunlit horizon.
How the autumn wind wheezes
And warm summer goes.
Leaves turn all crispy and dazzling gold.
Dawn is cheerful and gorgeous.
Autumn is here.

**Jacinta Cresswell (8)**
**Whitewater CE Primary School**

# Winter

Frosty icicles, glimmering snowflakes,
Winter is here at last.
Building a snowman on the grass,
Making white snow angels too.
Having a snowball fight on the field,
Having lots of fun.
Dragging the sledge up the slippery hill,
Then speeding all the way down.
Having hot, steaming cups of tea,
When you come in from the snow.
Huge, big dollops of apple crumble
And then your stomach is fit to explode!

**Elizabeth Carruthers  (8)**
**Whitewater CE Primary School**


# Autumn

Caramel brown, orangey yellow,
Golden brown and red.
Watch the conkers fall on the ground
That are half-open like an oyster.

**Rebecca Stephen  (7)**
**Whitewater CE Primary School**


# My Autumn Poem

Autumn is . . .
Conkers bolting down like thunder,
Birds twittering in the trees,
Golden brown, crisp-like leaves,
Swirling in the breeze.
Colourful rainbows,
Amber trees,
Squirrels collecting nuts,
Scurrying over crunchy leaves.

**Sam Hewlett  (9)**
**Whitewater CE Primary School**

# Winter Poem

Dripping icicles everywhere
Dancing snowflakes swirling and glistening,
Settling on the ground
Where hungry squirrels dig for their winter nuts.
Robins fluff up their feathers,
Keeping warm.
Holly leaves with their bright red berries.
In the town, chimneys smoke and lights
Twinkle through the windows.
Winter is such a lovely time.

**Catherine Ollerhead  (7)**
**Whitewater CE Primary School**

# Autumn

Crispy, crunchy, crackly autumn.
The wind makes the leaves swoop in the sky.
All the different colours flickering in the air,
Red, yellow, gold,
Orange and green.

**Charlie Stephen  (8)**
**Whitewater CE Primary School**

# Christmas

Christmas' face is old and hairy,
His mouth is like slivers of ice.
Roaming around the village,
In and out of the houses,
Shining as he goes.
Trees twinkling in his light,
Mischievous elves skipping around his feet,
Angels sing as he comes to town,
Snow falls on his cloak.

**Thomas White  (11)**
**Whitewater CE Primary School**

# Christmas

Christmas was in your stocking,
Now he's going down the stairs.
His angelic little eyes looking here and there,
Looking for the front door.
Still going down the stairs,
Leaving Christmas presents for the children who live there.

He stumbles down the pathway,
To the house next door.
As he goes, he can hear the joyfulness
Of the house he was last at.

**Elizabeth Floyd (10)**
**Whitewater CE Primary School**


# Christmas

C hristmas is like a white blanket all over the land.
H e has a long, dark green cloak for winter.
R eindeer walk slowly and gently to their houses.
I vy for his long arms.
S hortening days mean he must work through the night.
T he snow in his footprints from his cold feet.
M any people enjoy this time.
A ngels are above the clouds and the clouds are his hair.
S nowy owls fly silently around.

**Nicholas Cade (10)**
**Whitewater CE Primary School**

# My Autumn Poem

A glimpse of a squirrel, jumping from tree to tree,
A sight of a rabbit that I can see.
Scuttle of a deer, timid and shy,
Pouncing away up into the sky.
Coffee-brown acorns flying and floating,
Like a shower of fiery leaves.
A cloudburst of raindrops falling and flowing,
With a howl of the wind.
Ruby-red berries that I can see,
Birds pecking away, away.
An echo of my voice
With a flow of the wind.

**Max Davies  (10)**
**Whitewater CE Primary School**


# Autumn

Trees whispering to one another, *autumn is here.*
Howling winds showering crisp, gold leaves
                to the damp, muddy floor.
Juicy blackberries getting much sweeter.
Deer grazing on the cold, misty mornings.
Bright-eyed owls hooting as they look for food.
Hedgehogs gathering ruby-red leaves
             to snuggle down for winter.
The air is looping in the sky.
Rivers trickling down the stones.

**Ryan Compton  (9)**
**Whitewater CE Primary School**

# Snow Queen

I come in the night,
My kingdom awaits,
To turn the world to white,
For bright colours I hate.

The equipment I need,
My wand and crown,
The country I lead,
Is white, never brown.

Snow, my mystical blanket,
I inflict upon the land,
The puddles I turn to ice,
With a flick of my hand.

At the end of the night,
When my job is done,
My kingdom is white,
At the rise of the sun.

**Georgie White (10)**
**Whitewater CE Primary School**


# Winter Poem

The wind creeps in and helps Jack Frost
But does it at a terrible cost
The wind, rain, sleet and snow
All begins to shine and glow
The animals store and shiver
As the sky sprinkles caster sugar
And flakes of snow in the river's steady flow.

**Caitlin O'Sullivan (9)**
**Whitewater CE Primary School**

# My Winter Poem

The snow comes down, so freezing cold,
With hungry birds becoming tame and bold.
The blanket of snow, laid out on the ground,
Tame birds in the trees not making a sound.
Icicles hanging off the trees,
Tingling and melting in the breeze.
Frost climbing up the stems of flowers,
Reaching the petal and then it devours.
Jack Frost paints the windows white and grey
And like a flash of lightning, he flies away.
Boys and girls playing in the snow,
When the bell rings, into school they go.
Turkey for dinner on Christmas Day,
Children shout hip, hip, hooray!
Autumn is gone, it's far away
And Jack Frost comes to play.

**Sam Drew (8)**
**Whitewater CE Primary School**


# Winter

Land of whiteness all around us,
Crunchy snow as we play,
Fires glowing, chimneys smoking,
Frosty patterns and transparent icicles,
Swirling snowflakes melting to the ground,
Settling in the gutters,
Dripping, cold sheets of ice.
Icy lanes as we drive,
Gleaming icicles, dripping icicles,
Winter is gone!

**Heather Marnoch (8)**
**Whitewater CE Primary School**

# Everything Lost

Wendy was a young girl
From nineteen eighty-three
She loved to keep her secrets
Safe from you and me.

She wrote an important document
Especially for the Queen
She kept it safely hidden
It was never to be seen.

Then an enormous fire broke out
While she was sound asleep
But when she found her document
She sat down and began to weep.

Then she got so angry
And started to shout and scream
'I don't want to live in this world
So please let me leave.'

Then she fell into the fire
Underneath the blazing sun
All hope for our planet
Had left and finally gone.

**Dominique Cooper  (9)**
**Whitewater CE Primary School**


# Winter

Looking out of the window,
Icicles glitter and gleam
Children blowing out hot, hot air
Like dragons full of steam.

Children building snowmen
Frozen ponds like glass
Icicles are dripping down
On the stiff and frosty grass.

**Oliver Bushnell  (9)**
**Whitewater CE Primary School**

# Lost Molly

Molly is a cuddly cat
She's tortoiseshell you see
Her eyes are like green emeralds
She's lovely as can be.

One day we let her out to play
In the garden where she could run
Where she could bounce and hop around
Where she could have lots of fun.

We called her in for food we did
We called her loud and clear
Molly the cat we could not find
She was definitely not here.

Days and days we searched and searched
But Molly was not there
Just then one day we saw her appear
In the biggest tree just there.

**Hannah Cutler  (9)**
**Whitewater CE Primary School**


# Winter

Frost forming on windows
Ice glistening on roads
Icicles gleaming, shining in the sun
Sharpening as more water forms
Frosty, breezy winds
Sparkling snowflakes swirling down from the sky
Chimneys smoking
As children have snowball fights
As others laugh at them.

**Ben White  (8)**
**Whitewater CE Primary School**

# The Ballad Of Old Snap (Dog)

Snap and I were playing,
As happy as happy can be,
She loved to kill and kill some more,
She was a great friend to me.

I was playing in the bales with Snap one day,
She climbed on up ahead,
Suddenly, down a pigeon fell,
I looked and it was dead.

'Good girl, Snap, good girl,
Come on down to me,
You've killed a pigeon, well done,
Come on . . . let me see.'

But one day we walked up the road,
Old Snap ran on ahead,
Suddenly, we heard a yelp,
Old Snap was lying dead.

Mum picked snap up,
I saw her hard, crystal eyes.
That was it, I'd had enough
And tears burst out my eyes.

So there Snap was lying,
Her soul up, up and away,
Hoping I would see her,
Up there some other day.

**Jack Mitchell  (10)**
**Whitewater CE Primary School**

# A Winter Poem

Icicles dropping from frosty rooftops
Snow is falling from tree to tree
Animals hiding from the weather
Icy snowflakes fall from the sky.

Children playing in the frost
Chilly air fills the sky
Bare trees scattered around
Stretching their branches high.

Fairies dance like snowflakes high
Snowmen stand and dance around
Dripping webs from snowy trees
You can hear winter in the breeze.

**Sian Nabbs (10)**
**Whitewater CE Primary School**


# Winter

Winter, the coldest time of year,
Sparkling patterns all around
Glistening icicles shimmering bright,
Birds gone to foreign countries,
Snow on the windowpanes,
Cats by the fire so cosy and warm,
Fires flaming to and fro.

**Emily Belcher (8)**
**Whitewater CE Primary School**